THE ICELANDIC LANGUAGE

BY
STEFÁN KARLSSON

TRANSLATED BY
RORY McTURK

VIKING SOCIETY FOR NORTHERN RESEARCH
UNIVERSITY COLLEGE LONDON
2004

© 2004 Stefán Karlsson

ISBN: 978 0 903521 61 1

Reprinted with minor corrections 2013

Printed by Short Run Press Limited, Exeter

Preface

'Tungan', the work translated here, first appeared as a chapter in *Íslensk þjóðmenning*, vol. VI (Reykjavík: Þjóðsaga, 1989), 1–54, and has since been republished, with minor alterations and additions (including the numbering of sections and subsections) in *Stafkrókar* (2000; see Bibliography), 19–75. The present translation incorporates the changes made in the 2000 version, even though my work on it was mainly done in 1997–99.

Stefán Karlsson kindly gave me an offprint of 'Tungan' in September 1995. The idea of translating it first occurred to me in the spring of 1997, and I am grateful to Örnólfur Thorsson, who was Visiting Fellow in Icelandic Studies at the University of Leeds in 1996–97, for help and advice in the early stages of my work on the translation. I had completed about half of it (to the end of section 1, 'The language itself') by the summer of 1998, and translated the remainder during my year as Visiting Professor at Vanderbilt University, Nashville, Tennessee, in 1998–99. The translation has since been read in draft by Richard Perkins, Peter Foote, Desmond Slay, Michael Barnes, Peter Orton, and finally Stefán himself, to all of whom I am deeply grateful for their comments and suggestions. I am particularly grateful to Stefán for his acceptance and support of the idea of publishing this work of his in English, and for the thoroughness with which he read and commented on the translation. My thanks are also due to Andrew Wawn, whose recognition of the value of 'Tungan' for teaching purposes encouraged me to bring my work on it to completion, and to Anthony Faulkes for the care with which he has prepared the translation for the press.

In its original form this work was, of course, intended for Icelandic readers, in whom knowledge of the pronunciation of Modern Icelandic could easily be assumed. With this in mind I have given in the text a minimal amount of additional information about Icelandic pronunciation, most especially in subsection 1.2.1, where Stefán compares the vowel sounds of Old Icelandic with those of Modern Icelandic. I have slightly reduced and reordered the information given in subsections 1.1.1–3, and have added English translations of words and phrases in languages other than English that are referred to in the text; I have also parsed Icelandic words where it seemed to me helpful to do so. What is offered here is, however, a translation rather than an adaptation; I have not otherwise ventured to alter Stefán's treatment of his material in any way, and only hope, indeed, that I have represented it with reasonable accuracy. Any errors of translation are, of course, entirely my responsibility.

R. McT.
Leeds, April 2004

Abbreviations

acc.	accusative
adj., adjs	adjective(s)
adv.	adverb
comp.	comparative
dat.	dative
f.	feminine
gen.	genitive
indic.	indicative
inf.	infinitive
m.	masculine
ModIcel.	Modern Icelandic
n.	neuter
nom.	nominative
OldIcel.	Old Icelandic
pers.	person
pl.	plural
poss.	possessive
pp.	past participle
pres.	present
pret.	preterite
sg.	singular
subj.	subjunctive

Note: In the numbered extracts printed at the foot of pages 38–63 with facing translations, and illustrating different stages in the history of Icelandic and its spelling, the following editorial practices have been adopted: italics indicate expansion of abbreviations, pointed brackets ‹ › mark off letters that have been supplied in cases of omission, and the asterisk * marks words in which errors of other kinds have been emended. The oblique strokes in extracts 10 and 12, on the other hand, correspond to punctuation marks in the original texts.

Contents

Introduction 7
1. The language itself 8
2. Orthography 39
3. One language 64
Bibliography 67
General index 75
Index of words and phrases 79

Introduction

This book surveys the main developments in the history of the Icelandic language and the major changes in orthography from one period to another.

The sound system of the earliest Icelandic, developments in the vocalic system, and numerous combinative changes are outlined. It should be noted that not all the innovations described have affected the whole country; some indeed were limited in distribution and did not achieve permanence.

Some major changes in inflexion are also described, with due account taken of the fact that inflexional differences between Old and Modern Icelandic are slight, not least because nineteenth-century purists set their face against a number of levelling-out developments which were by then well advanced.

Vocabulary and lexical changes are discussed, with special reference to foreign influences and native resistance to them. Many words were introduced into the language as a result of the conversion to Christianity, some of them loan-words and some of them neologisms. Loan-words then and later came by various routes; Low German vocabulary by way of Norwegian and Danish is a large element, especially evident in religious writings of the Reformation period and in the language of state officials. Loan-words had, however, a limited spread among the population at large, and in some quarters a purist policy was consciously pursued, especially from the mid-eighteenth century onwards. Since then many neologisms have been created, mostly on the basis of native stems.

The section on orthography begins with the first attempts to write Icelandic using the roman alphabet. In the mid-twelfth century the author of the First Grammatical Treatise devised a remarkably complete set of rules for spelling the Icelandic of his time and though these were influential in the centuries that ensued they were never followed to the letter. Practice varied in denoting individual sounds and no scribe was entirely consistent in his usage. The section ends with a discussion of attempts to find a fixed orthography for the language. These began in earnest in the second half of the eighteenth century and continued in the nineteenth, when a strong archaising tendency gradually became more and more dominant.

Finally, it is observed that in general the differences between Old and Modern Icelandic are few and small, and that dialectal differences are virtually non-existent. Explanations of this conservatism are found in the exceptional literary heritage and practice of the Icelanders, in the fact that communications, and not least the movement of people, between different parts of the country were constant, and in the self-conscious desire of the Icelanders to preserve their ancient language and the link it gave them to their past.

1. The language itself

1.1.1 Related tongues

Icelandic is a Scandinavian or North Germanic language, belonging to the Indo-European language family.[1] As far as we can tell, Iceland was settled in the late ninth century, and before and after that period Scandinavians carved runes on wood or stone. Although most of the preserved inscriptions are short, they provide important information about the language of the Scandinavian kinsmen and forebears of present-day native speakers of Icelandic. Significant information can also be gained from early Germanic loan-words in Finnish which still remain, little changed, in that language.

1.1.2 Proto-Scandinavian changes

The settlement of Iceland was preceded by a period in which great linguistic changes took place among Scandinavian speakers. The most influential of these were vowel syncope, i.e., the loss of short vowels in unstressed positions, and vowel mutation and the diphthongisation called breaking, both of which sometimes took place in association with vowel syncope. The results of these sound changes are seen in e.g. *lātiʀ > lætr*, third pers. sg. pres. indic. of *láta* 'to let', i.e., 'to allow'; *briūtiʀ > brýtr*, third pers. sg. pres. indic. of *brjóta* 'to break'; *berga > bjarg* 'boulder', *bergu > bjǫrg*, nom. and acc. pl. of *bjarg*. Sometimes other changes were also involved, with outcomes that are still further removed from ancient forms, e.g. *fanhan > fá* 'to obtain', *sehwan > séa > sjá* 'to see'. Vowel mutation and breaking did not follow exactly the same pattern throughout the Scandinavian speech area. Resulting discrepancies are among the earliest features which distinguish the Northern languages one from another and lead to the distinction between East and West Scandinavian, the former comprising Danish and Swedish, the latter Norwegian and the languages of the colonies settled chiefly from Norway in parts of the British Isles and the islands of the Atlantic.[2]

1.1.3 Origins

Icelandic is thus a West Scandinavian language. It contains, however, a handful of words of Celtic origin: a few personal names, *Kjartan* and *Njáll*, for example, and the occasional place-name like *Dímon* 'twin-peak';

---

[1] Hreinn Benediktsson 1964b; Kristján Árnason 1980a, 22–24, and 1980b, 133–38.
[2] Bandle 1973, 24–36, 52–56.

further a number of words associated with husbandry, once in common use but now mostly rare, the word *sofn* 'kiln for drying lyme-grass seed', for instance, found in Skaftafellssýsla and originally meaning 'fire' (lymegrass seed was dried over a fire in a *sofnhús* 'fire-house'); or *slafak* 'watercotton', first used of edible seaweed. Some of these Celtic words are not known in medieval texts but only in the later language.[3] Nevertheless, they were probably all brought to Iceland by Celts among the first settlers.[4] Whatever the precise number of Celtic words so introduced, their meagre survival strongly suggests that the most influential strand of speech among the settlers was that of a Scandinavian ruling class.

The earliest preserved written Icelandic sources date from the second half of the twelfth century. At that time there was very little difference between Icelandic and Norwegian, particularly West Norwegian, but the divide between the languages increased in the thirteenth and still more in the fourteenth century. Certain sound-changes unparalleled in Norwegian did take place in Icelandic, but it was Norwegian which underwent more profound alteration, not least in a large simplification of its inflexional system. In the mid-twelfth century the author of the First Grammatical Treatise wrote that the English and Icelanders are 'of one language', but nevertheless saw it as his task to create 'an alphabet for us Icelanders'.[5] (See further § 2.1 below.) In the earliest writings Scandinavian speech as a whole is called 'dǫnsk tunga' ('Danish tongue'), and in the thirteenth century sometimes 'norrœn tunga' ('Nordic tongue'). Later it was the latter expression, or its equivalent *norrœna* '(Old) Norse', which was used of the language of Norwegians and those people whose ancestors came from Norway. Later again the same expressions were used solely to refer to Icelandic, a practice which continued well into the seventeenth century. The word *norræna* is used, for example, on the title-page of Oddur Gottskálksson's translation of the New Testament, published in 1540.[6]

1.2. Pronunciation and sound changes

It is possible to gain some idea of the pronunciation of early Icelandic and of the changes it underwent. This is particularly true in cases where a phonetic distinction would lead to a semantic distinction (cf. e.g. the vowels

---

[3] Hermann Pálsson 1952 and 1996, 150–207; Helgi Guðmundsson 1959, 1960, 1969, 1970 and 1997, 121–99; de Vries 1962, xxi–xxii; Jakob Benediktsson 1964, 88–95.
[4] Stefán Aðalsteinsson 1987.
[5] Hreinn Benediktsson 1972, 208.
[6] Jóhannes L. L. Jóhannsson 1929; Karker 1977.

in *mál* : *mal* : *mel*) (*mál*, n., = either 'speech', etc., or 'measure', 'time', etc.; *mal* is acc. sg. of *malr*, m., 'knapsack'; *mel* is acc. sg. of *melr*, m., 'lyme-grass' or 'gravel-bank'). It is harder to judge the exact pronunciation of individual sounds in the old language but we can reach a close approximation with some confidence.

The pronunciation of Icelandic before the age of sound-recording can be deduced from various kinds of evidence. The most important are the rhymes and other metrical features of verse composition, the orthography of written texts, and contemporary descriptions of speech. Among descriptions of this last sort the First Grammatical Treatise is by far the most significant.[7] Comparison with related languages also plays a part.

Modern Icelandic spelling closely resembles 'normalised' Old Icelandic spelling, but there is no doubt that, in relative terms, there are very large differences in pronunciation between the early language and that of the present day. This is particularly true of the vowel sounds; consonants have undergone only minor change.[8]

1.2.1 The oldest-known vowel system

Vowels are commonly divided into front and back vowels according to the tongue's position when articulating them; into close, mid and open vowels according to how far the mouth is open; and into rounded and unrounded vowels according to the way the mouth is shaped in uttering them. Using these categories nine vowels may be distinguished in the language of the early centuries of the Icelandic settlement:

	Front		Back	
	Unrounded	Rounded	Unrounded	Rounded
Close	i	y		u
Mid	e	ø		o
Open	ę		a	ǫ

Thus *i* was a front, close, unrounded vowel, like *í* in ModIcel.; *e* was front, mid, and unrounded, much like *i* in ModIcel.; *ę* was front, open, and unrounded, like ModIcel. *e*; *y* was a front, close, rounded vowel, pronounced like Danish *y*—in ModIcel. it is now pronounced like *i*; *ø* was a front, mid (or between mid and close, i.e., half-close), rounded vowel, like ModIcel. *ö* or *u*; *a* was a back, open, unrounded vowel, pronounced just as it is today; *u* was a back, close, rounded vowel, like ModIcel. *ú*; *o* was a back, mid, rounded vowel, more open than ModIcel.

[7] Hreinn Benediktsson 1972.
[8] Hreinn Benediktsson 1962b, 486–91, and 1964c.

THE ICELANDIC LANGUAGE

ú but closer than ModIcel. *o*; and *ǫ* was a back, open, rounded vowel, with a pronunciation like that of ModIcel. *o*.

Other distinguishing features were length—vowels were long or short— and nasality; depending on their phonological inheritance, pronunciation of long vowels was either through the nose or through the mouth. This meant that in the earliest stage of development known to us Icelandic had 27 vowels and 3 diphthongs. The diphthongs were *au*, pronounced like English *ow* in 'how', with articulation involving a tongue-movement from the position of *a* to that of *u*; *ei*, pronounced like English *ay* in 'say', with articulation involving movement from *e* or *ę* to *i*; and finally *ey*, whose articulation involved movement from *e*, *ę* or *ø* to *y*.

1.2.2 Changes in the vowel system

As early as the twelfth century, and even earlier in some cases, the number of distinct vowels decreased: short *e* and short *ę* fell together very early,[9] all long vowels came to be pronounced without nasalisation, and long *ǫ* (*ǭ*) fell together with long *a* (*á*) if it was articulated orally, with long *o* (*ó*) if it was articulated nasally. By about 1200 the number of vowels was 16, plus the 3 diphthongs.

In the following centuries the number of distinct vowels decreased still further. Distinction between short *ø* and *ǫ* was becoming blurred around 1200, and in some contexts *ø* was unrounded (e.g. *øxi* > *exi* 'axe'); unrounding of long *ø* (normalized as *ǿ* or *æ*) began about the middle of the thirteenth century with the result that it fell together with long *ę* (traditionally written *æ*). Finally short and long *y* (*y* and *ý*), independently and in the diphthong *ey*, were unrounded, so that *y*, *ý*, *ey* fell together with *i*, *í*, *ei* respectively. This unrounding began in the latter part of the fifteenth century and was completed in the seventeenth. In a few words, however, ModIcel. *u* (a front, half-close rounded vowel) is often heard where *y* (a front, close rounded vowel) originally occurred, e.g. in *spyrja* 'to ask' and *kyrr* 'still' (adj.) (*spurja* and *kjur(r)*).[10] When these changes had taken place the monophthongs and diphthongs of Icelandic had been reduced to 14 in all.

Linguistic change is a gradual process. The changes in the Icelandic vowel system must have taken generations to become established throughout the population.

[9] Hreinn Benediktsson 1964a.
[10] Björn K. Þórólfsson 1929b, 240–43; Leijström 1934; Sveinn Bergsveinsson 1955; Hreinn Benediktsson 1965, 56–73, and 1977; Guðvarður Már Gunnlaugsson 1994.

The vowel system was affected not just by the simplification so far described. There were also cases in which one or both of two vowels that originally differed from one another in length alone, such as *i* and *í*, changed in such a way that length ceased to be the only feature distinguishing them. Short vowels became more open in pronunciation, only *a* retaining its old value. (A further development is seen in the vowels of unstressed endings: *e* and *o* in the earliest writings give way to *i* and *u* in the thirteenth century.[11]) The vowels represented by *í*, *ú* and *ý* (as long as this last existed) retained their old value, but other long vowels were diphthongised. Long *e* (*é*) acquired an articulation which may be expressed as *ie*, with the tongue moving from the position of *i* to that of *e*. Later the initial *i* sound became a palatal glide.[12] *æ* (which had developed from both early *ę* and *œ*), *á*, and *ó* also remain in the alphabet but are pronounced as diphthongs, as *ai*, *au*, and *ou* respectively. Of the three early diphthongs, *ei* is pronounced as it always was, and *au* developed a pronunciation *øi*, probably through an intermediate stage *øu*; the sound *au* now has is comparable to the value of *ey* before this fell together with *ei* as a result of unrounding.[13]

Distinction of vowels had originally been by length alone, but once these qualitative changes emerged, the vowel-length system underwent radical change. This development, often known as the quantity shift, must in the main have run its course in the sixteenth century. Before the shift a stressed syllable was short if it contained a short vowel followed by a short (= single) consonant (e.g. *bak* 'back' (noun)). It was long if it consisted of a long vowel followed by one or more consonants (e.g. *áma* 'barrel'; *hrædd*, nom. f. sg. and nom. and acc. n. pl. of adj. *hræddr* 'afraid'; *týnd*, nom. f. sg. and nom. and acc. n. pl. of pp. *týndr* 'lost'), or of a short vowel followed by a long (= double) consonant (e.g. *enni* 'forehead') or by a consonant cluster (e.g. *seld*, nom. f. sg. and nom. and acc. n. pl. of pp. *seldr* 'sold'). Length could vary in stressed syllables ending in a vowel, though when such a syllable is followed by a final vowel (as in *búa* 'to dwell') it was counted a short syllable in verse. When the quantity shift had taken place, every vowel, whether monophthong or diphthong, in a stressed syllable could be short or long, with the variation depending on the sounds that followed it. Vowels are now long in final position and when followed by a short (single) consonant (e.g. *reka* 'to drive'), by no consonant (e.g. *búa* (see above)), or by the consonants *p, t, k, s* when

---

[11] Cf. Hreinn Benediktsson 1962a.
[12] Jóhannes L. L. Jóhannsson 1924, 11–19; Björn K. Þórólfsson 1929b, 232–40.
[13] Hreinn Benediktsson 1959; Stefán Karlsson 1981, 277–79.

combined with a following *j* (e.g. *lepja* 'to lap up'), *v* (e.g. *uppgötva* 'to discover'; *tvisvar* 'twice') or *r* (e.g. *dekra* 'to pamper'). They are short when followed by a long consonant (e.g. *banna* 'to forbid'; *urr* 'dog's growl') or by consonant clusters other than those just specified (e.g. *banda* 'to wave'; *urð* 'scree').[14] With the quantity shift every stressed syllable was long but the degree of stress could be amplified by drawing out the pronunciation of a long vowel or the enunciation of the consonant following a short vowel.

One further change in the vowels needs mention: the confusion of quality known as *flámæli* 'open-mouthed speech', for which the wider term *hljóðvilla* 'sound-confusion' is sometimes also used. When this began is uncertain but it was mostly in evidence in the earlier part of the twentieth century and especially common in eastern and south-western Iceland. Speakers affected by *flámæli* make little or no distinction between *i* and *e* or between *u* and *ö*, particularly if these vowels are to be pronounced long (*u* and *ö* being normally or 'correctly' pronounced as front, rounded vowels, though *ö* as more open than *u*). Since these are among the commonest vowels in the language, it is clear that universal adoption of the pronunciation would have led to a further reduction of the Icelandic vowel set. The result would have been words distinguished in spelling but not in speech in greater profusion than any of the older, comparable changes had brought about.[15]

1.2.3 Combinative vowel change

As well as the changes affecting the vowel system as a whole, others took place that can be called combinative, i.e., the affected vowels underwent change in specific phonetic environments. Some of these changes have not been generally accepted, others are restricted to certain parts of the country.

The earliest change of this kind began before the end of the twelfth century. It involved the lengthening of a back vowel before *l* when this was followed by any consonant other than a dental (e.g. *ulfr* > *úlfr* 'wolf'; *halmr* > *hálmr* 'straw'; *folk* > *fólk* 'people'), while words like *valda* 'to cause' and *holt* 'hillock' were unaffected. There are, however, cases of this lengthening taking place before other clusters with *l* in them (e.g. *hals* > *háls* 'neck'; *álnir*, pl. of *alin* 'ell').[16]

---

[14] Björn K. Þórólfsson 1929a; Hreinn Benediktsson 1967–68; Kristján Árnason 1980c.
[15] Stefán Einarsson 1932, 53–54; Björn Guðfinnsson 1947, 24–27, and 1964, 81–117.
[16] Noreen 1923, 109–10; Ásgeir Bl. Magnússon 1981.

By about 1300 short vowels before *ng* and *nk* were in the process of change. Close vowels were lengthened (*ing* > *íng, yng* > *ýng, ung* > *úng*); the rest were dipthongised (*eng* > *eing, öng* > *aung*).[17] In the Vestfirðir, however, the latter are still pronounced as monophthongs.[18] (The examples given here are word-elements rather than words, though *ung* may be identified as the nom. sg. f. and nom. and acc. pl. n. of *ungr* 'young', and *eng* as the noun meaning 'meadow'.)

A rather similar change took place later, mainly in the fifteenth century, when a short vowel occurred before *g* followed by *i* or *j*. In this combination the *g* became a palatal glide (ModIcel. *j*) and a preceding close short vowel, *i* or *y*, was lengthened (in speech but not in spelling, e.g. *stigi* 'ladder'; *lygi* 'lie' (noun)), while other short vowels became diphthongs, with tongue-movement from the vowel's ordinary position towards that of front, close *i* (*í* in ModIcel.). The change can be heard in e.g. *daginn*, acc. sg. of *dagurinn* 'the day'; *megi*, as in the third pers. sg. and pl. pres. subj. of *mega* 'be permitted'; *bogi* 'bow (for shooting arrows)'; *lögin* 'the law(s)'.[19] This change has not been fully effected in south-eastern Iceland.[20]

Some vowels altered their quality after *v*. Probably the first such change was that of *vé* to *væ*, which can be found already in the thirteenth century. Only a few words were affected, particularly those in which the vowel was followed by *l* or *r*;[21] thus the pronoun *vér* 'we' had *vær* as a common variant for centuries, and *vélindi* and *vælindi* (both meaning 'gullet') remain variants to this day. The change of *vá* to *vo* (e.g. *váði* > *voði* 'danger', *svá* > *svo* 'so') began in the first half of the fourteenth century. *vó* may have been an intermediate stage in this development but in any case the resultant rounded vowel consistently remained long until the time of the quantity shift. The change was a general one and virtually every word with *vá* in the modern language is either an analogical form (*kváðu* '(they) recited', *sváfu* '(they) slept') or lifted from the old language (e.g. *vá* 'damage', 'danger', and compounds with this word as an element).[22] The rounding of *ve* to *vö* began about 1400, but *vö* has become established in only a few

---

[17] Noreen 1923, 110; Jóhannnes L. L. Jóhannsson 1924, 19–24; Bandle 1956, 28, 31, 33, 45–46, 78–80; Stefán Karlsson 1981, 258–59, 279–82.
[18] Björn Guðfinnsson 1964, 118–33.
[19] Björn K. Þórólfsson 1925, xii–xiii, xviii; Bandle 1956, 28–29, 35–36, 46–47; Kristján Árnason 1980b, 123.
[20] Björn Guðfinnsson 1964, 134–43; Ingólfur Pálmason 1983, 37–41; Kristján Árnason and Höskuldur Þráinsson 1983.
[21] Kock 1895, 140–41.
[22] Björn K. Þórólfsson 1925, xi–xii; Bandle 1956, 41; Hreinn Benediktsson 1979.

words (*kvöld* 'evening', *tvöfaldur* 'double' (adj.)); in exceptional cases the development was to *vo* (*hvolfa* 'to overturn', *hvolpur* 'puppy'). In the sixteenth century and later *vö* in words with comparatively little stress could become *vu* (*hvur, hvurninn*, variants respectively of *hver* 'who', 'which', 'what'; 'each'; and *hvernig* 'how').[23]

From about 1600 unrounding of *jö* to *je* becomes perceptible. This was much in evidence in the seventeenth century but in most cases the old form has been restored (e.g. *mjög* > *mjeg* > *mjög* 'very' (adv.), *sjö* > *sje* > *sjö* 'seven'). There are still a few variant forms (*fjögur* : *fjegur*, n. of *fjórir* 'four'; *smjör* : *smjer* 'butter' (noun)), and in one or two words *je* is the established form (*ófjeti*, n., 'scoundrel'< *ófjöt*, n. pl., 'impropriety'; *stjel*, n., 'tail (of bird)' < *stjölr*, m., 'rump').[24]

When a consonant other than *r* was followed by *r*, either in a final position or before another consonant, an epenthetic *u* developed before the *r* (*fagr* > *fagur* 'beautiful', *fegrð* > *fegurð* 'beauty'). This inserted vowel sound can be first observed about 1300 and seems to have been universally established by the middle of the fifteenth century.[25]

A break in pronunciation between two adjacent vowels that do not make a diphthong is called hiatus. If the first of two such vowels was long and stressed and the second relatively unstressed, then in certain circumstances they ceased to exist as two syllables and became one, e.g. *séa* > *sjá* 'to see', *féhús* > *fjós* 'cowshed' (with loss of medial *h*). This development had taken place before the time of our earliest writings. In certain other circumstances the vowels remained as two syllables, while in others again the second vowel was assimilated. Words in which the vowels have remained as two syllables include the following: *fái*, as in e.g. the third pers. sg. pres. subj. of *fá* 'to obtain'; *búi* 'inhabitant'; *rói*, as in the third pers. sg. pres. subj. of *róa* 'to row'; *búa* 'to dwell'; *róa* 'to row'. Words in which the second vowel has been assimilated, on the other hand, include: *fáa* > *fá* 'to obtain' (also acc. pl. m. (in OldIcel.) of *fár* 'few') and *fáom* > *fóum* (by *u*-mutation) > *fóm* > *fám*, first pers. pl. pres. indic. (in OldIcel.) of *fá* 'to obtain' (also dat. pl. all genders (in OldIcel.) of *fár* 'few'). In the fifteenth century and later analogy with other words of the same conjugation or declension led to the restoration of the relatively unstressed second vowel in forms like those just mentioned. Thus, for instance, the

---

[23] Jóhannes L. L. Jóhannsson 1924, 43–44; Björn K. Þórólfsson 1925, xiii; Bandle 1956, 42–43, 60–63, 81; Stefán Karlsson 1981, 260–61.
[24] Björn K. Þórólfsson 1925, xix–xx; Bandle 1956, 90.
[25] Jón Þorkelsson 1863; Stefán Karlsson 1982, 59.

infinitive *fá* remained; but *fá*, acc. pl. m. of adj. *fár*, reacquired its ancient form, *fáa*; and *fám*, first pers. pl. pres. indic. of the verb *fá* and dat. pl. of adj. *fár*, once more became *fáum*.[26]

A hiatus change which took place in the fourteenth century and later can be observed in compound words. If the first element ended in a short vowel with little stress and the second element began with a vowel (or with *h* followed by a vowel), the final vowel of the first element was lost (and sometimes an *h* introducing the second element). The spelling of some words shows this development fully established (e.g. the place-name *Skálholt* < *Skálaholt*, and *fasteign* 'real estate' < *fastaeign*); in others the vowel is still spelt and may sometimes be heard in speech (e.g. the place-names *Blönd(u)ós* and *Litl(ih)amar*). Omission of the last sound or sounds of a word (apocope) often occurs when the next word follows without pause and begins with a vowel (*inn(i)undir*, as in the phrase *innundir hjá einhverjum* 'in favour with someone'; *farð(u) ekki* 'don't go'). The rhythm of verse often requires this kind of elision, and it is natural in unstilted everyday speech.

1.2.4 The consonant system

While it may be said that the ModIcel. consonant system is much the same as that of the early language, considerable changes have taken place in the pronunciation of individual consonants in specific phonetic environments. The chief developments are seen in the change of fricatives (continuant consonants produced by forcing air through the mouth along with some narrowing of the vocal tract) to their corresponding stops; and in the unvoicing of consonants previously voiced (like the *l* in *mjólk* 'milk' (noun) as pronounced in northern Iceland).

Consonants may be broadly classified according to the position of their articulation in the mouth; thus for Icelandic:[27]

	Labial	Dental	Velar
Fortis stops	p	t	k
Lenis stops	b	d	g
Fricatives	f	þ/ð, s	g
Nasals	m	n	n(+g/k)
Lateral and trill		l, r	

This table does not include the sounds usually represented by *v* and *j*. At first these had the character of what are called semivowels, each marking

[26] Noreen 1923, 115–18; Bandle 1956, 39–40, 69–70.
[27] Hreinn Benediktsson 1965, 73; Kristján Árnason 1980b, 89–125.

a transition in pronunciation between a vowel and a consonant, and with a value like that of ModIcel. *ú* and *í* respectively. *v* soon acquired more of a consonantal character, that of voiced *f*, but in verse initial *j* continued for centuries to alliterate with vowels. *v* is now a voiced labio-dental fricative (like intervocalic *f* in *hafa* 'to have'), and *j* a palatal glide. *h* is also absent from the table. In Proto-Scandinavian it must have been a voiceless velar fricative, as it still is in initial *hv* among speakers who retain this form and have not gone over to *kv*. Before another consonant *h* signifies little more than the unvoicing of the consonant in question (*hj, hl, hn, hr*). Before a vowel it is a fricative with a narrowing of the middle or back region of the mouth.[28]

A velar variant of *n* has also always existed in words where *n* is immediately followed by *g* or *k* (*hanga* 'to hang (about)'; *hanka*, oblique sg. cases and acc. and gen. pl. of *hanki* 'handle', 'loop' (noun)).

The difference between *p, t, k* and *b, d, g* in the oldest language is uncertain. We do not know, for instance, whether the latter trio were voiced. All of them are now voiceless. In initial position *p, t, k* are universally aspirated (e.g. *tala* 'to speak'), and the same pronunciation is heard in other positions from people who have the speech-habit called *harðmæli* 'hard speech'. These have the aspirated consonant when it occurs finally or before a vowel and is immediately preceded by another vowel or by a voiced consonant (*l, m, n* or *ð*) (e.g. *át* 'ate'; *vaka* 'to stay awake'; *hjálpa* 'to help'). When *p, t, k* are long (written double) or followed by another consonant, they are preaspirated (preceded by an *h*-like breath); examples with *p* are *uppi* 'above' (adv.) and *opna* 'to open'.

The velar consonants *k* and *g* (the latter whether stop or fricative) were palatalised before a front vowel already in the oldest language. When back and front vowels came to change their point of articulation in the period from about 1200 onward, however, the velar consonants remained unaffected. There is thus a distinction still made between *kjör* (< *kør* 'choice'), with palatal *k*, and *kör* (< *kǫr* '(sick)bed'), with velar *k*, even though *ö* in *kör* has long been a front vowel like the *ö* in *kjör*. In the same way velar *g* is retained in *gufa* 'steam' (noun and verb), for example, even though *u* is now a front vowel, while palatal *g* is retained in *gæfa* 'good luck', even though the first element in the *æ* diphthong is the back vowel *a*.

Fricative *f* has always been voiceless in initial position, and the same is true of *þ*, though with some exceptions. In medial and final position *f* and *g* have been variously voiced and voiceless according to their phonetic

[28] Höskuldur Þráinsson 1981.

context (*hafa* 'to have', *saga* '(hi)story' (voiced) : *haft, sagt,* nom. and acc. sg. n. of pp. of *hafa* and *segja* 'to say' respectively (unvoiced)). Voiced or voiceless pronunciation of *ð* in certain combinations (e.g. in *blaðka* 'leaf' (noun); *aðferð* 'method') is now a dialect marker.[29]

Nasal, lateral and trill consonants are both voiced and unvoiced in ModIcel. Since no distinction between the voiced and unvoiced variants has ever been made in spelling, we cannot determine the age of the voiceless kind. Voiced or voiceless pronunciation of *m, n* and *l* before *p, t* and *k* (as in *stampur* 'tub'; *vanta* 'to lack', 'to need'; *banka,* 'to knock'; *mjólk* 'milk' (noun)) is another distinguishing dialect feature.[30]

It is thought that in early Icelandic *n* and *l* were each pronounced both as a dental (as in ModIcel.) and as an alveolar or cacuminal. Probably dental *n* soon superseded its alveolar variant everywhere, but the dental and cacuminal forms of *l* continued to exist side by side until the seventeenth century.[31]

1.2.5 Various consonant changes

The written language and the evidence of rhymes in verse in particular show that at an early stage the labials *p, pp* and *f* before *t* were pronounced alike, and the same kind of merger before *t* was experienced by the velars *k, kk, g* and *gg*. Nevertheless, force of analogy often led to a spelling distinction between *p(p)t* and *ft* (e.g. *hleypt, slep(p)t, haft,* nom. and acc. sg. n. of pp. of *hleypa* 'to cause to move', *sleppa* 'to release', and *hafa* 'to have', respectively) and between *k(k)t* and *g(g)t* (*ríkt,* nom. and acc. sg. n. of *ríkr* 'rich'; *stök(k)t, lagt,* nom. and acc. sg. n. of pp. of *stökkva* 'to chase away' and *leggja* 'to place' respectively). Much the same is true of both these labials and velars when they occurred before *s*, as is demonstrated in the case of the latter group by the spelling *x* for *k(k)s* and *g(g)s*. Before *t* and *s* these labials and velars were probably pronounced as voiceless fricatives, as they are today: *f* as in *haft,* for example (see above), and *g* as in *sagt,* nom. and acc. sg. n. of pp. of *segja* 'to say'.[32]

The dentals *t(t)* and *d(d),* and to some extent *ð*, also came to be pronounced the same before *s* at an early period. The combination was presumably pronounced *ts* but was most often written *z,* though the spelling sometimes included the original dental (*broz* : *brotz,* i.e., *brots,* gen. sg. of

---

[29] Björn Guðfinnsson 1964, 17–43.
[30] Björn Guðfinnsson 1964, 17–43.
[31] Jakob Benediktsson 1960b.
[32] Hreinn Benediktsson 1965, 76–77, 79–80.

brot 'fracture'; *broz* : *broddz*, i.e., *brodds*, gen. sg. of *broddr* 'spike'). The clusters *lls* and *nns* developed in the same way as *lds*, *lts* and *nds*, but *ls* and *ns* did not, so that the pronunciation of e.g. *kolls* (written *kol(l)z*), gen. sg. of *kollr* 'head' (noun), differed from that of *kols* (written *kols*), gen. sg. of *kol* '(piece of) coal').[33] Otherwise no distinction was made between short and long consonants in consonant clusters. In time *z* lost its independent value and was (and is) pronounced the same as *s* when combined with another consonant or as *ss* in intervocalic positions (*bleza* > *blessa* 'to bless'). When this happened has been a matter of controversy but manuscript forms suggest that the change was not much in evidence before the sixteenth century.

Where a syllable with relatively little stress ended in *t* or *k* these stops became the fricatives *ð* and *g* respectively (*vit* > *við* 'we (two)', *blaðit* > *blaðið* 'the leaf'; *ek* > *eg* 'I', *mik* > *mig* 'me', *mjök* > *mjög* 'very' (adv.)). There is evidence for this change from as early as the thirteenth century.

Initial *kn* appears as *hn* in the fourteenth and fifteenth century but we do not know how far this was a general change. The modern language has various *kn-* words which are either survivals or revivals. In some cases variants exist in particular circumstances (*hné* 'knee', for instance, but *kné* in the idiom *koma einhverjum á kné* 'to bring someone to his knees', i.e., 'to defeat someone') or with different meanings (e.g. *hnöttur* 'the globe', *knöttur* 'ball').[34]

The fricatives *f*, *ð* and *g* became stops in various other consonant combinations than those noted above. Some such changes were under way in the thirteenth century or even earlier but most of them probably took place in the fourteenth century: before *l* and *n*, *f* became *b* (*efla* 'to strengthen', *nafn* 'name', pronounced *ebbla, nabbn* respectively) and before *ð* too (e.g. *hafði* (as in e.g. the third pers. sg. pret. indic. of *hafa* 'to have') pronounced *habbði*), though this last change may not have been universal—*bbð* for *fð* is still heard today but not in many localities.[35]

In some parts of the country *f* also became *b* after *l* and *r* (*kálfar* 'calves' (noun) > *kálbar*; *orf* 'scythe-handle' > *orb*), and traces of this pronunciation remained in northern and western Iceland down to the end of the nineteenth century.[36] When preceded by *p* or *k*, *ð* (*þ*) became *t* (*kippði* > *kippti*, as in

---

[33] Hoffory 1883, 79–96; Bandle 1956, 166–67, 173–79; Hreinn Benediktsson 1965, 74–76.
[34] Björn K. Þórólfsson 1925, xxxii; Halldór Halldórsson 1950, 66.
[35] Björn Guðfinnsson 1964, 144–70.
[36] Björn K. Þórólfsson 1925, xxvi–xxvii; Jón Helgason 1955b, x.

the third pers. sg. pret. of *kippa* 'to snatch'; *spekþ* > *spekt* 'wisdom'), but preceded by *l*, *n* or *m* it became *d* (*hulði* > *huldi*; *vanði* > *vandi*; *samði* > *samdi*, as in the third pers. sg. pret. indic. of *hylja* 'to hide', *venja* 'to accustom', and *semja* 'to adapt' respectively). *ð* also became *d* after a consonant pair with *l*, *m*, *n* as the first element, with the intervening element apparently lost in the process: *skelfði* > *skel(f)di*, *hengði* > *hen(g)di* (with velar *n* as in *hengja*), *kembði* > *kem(b)di*, as in the third pers. sg. pret. of *skelfa* 'to frighten', *hengja* 'to hang (up)' and *kemba* 'to comb' respectively.[37] In some localities *ð* also became *d* after *f*, *g* or *r* (*hafdi*, *sagdi*, *bardi*, as in the third pers. sg. pret. indic. of *hafa* 'to have', *segja* 'to say', and *berja* 'to beat' respectively); traces of this pronunciation are still found in northern and western Iceland.[38]

In early Icelandic *g* is thought to have been a stop only when initial (*gata* 'street'), or when long (*dögg* 'dew'), or in the combination *ng* (*anga* 'to smell sweet').[39] In ModIcel. it is now a stop in several other positions: after *f (v)*, *ð*, *m*, *l* and *r* (*göfga* 'to ennoble'; *blóðga* 'to cause to bleed'; *blómgast* 'to bloom'; *belg*, acc. sg. of *belgur* 'hide' (noun); *bjarg* 'boulder'). After *t*, *g* became *k* (*máttugur* 'powerful', but acc. sg. m. *máttkan*). *g* also became a stop before *n* and *l* as well as—at least in some dialects—before *ð* (*ögn* 'small particle', *negla* 'to nail', *sagði* as in the third pers. sg. pret. indic. of *segja* 'to say'; pronounced *öggn*, *neggla*, *saggði* respectively). The change before *ð* may indeed have taken place wherever *ð* did not become *d* in the same position. But the pronunciation of *ð* as a stop after voiced fricative *f* and *g* (*havdi*, *sagdi*) and of *f* and *g* as stops before *ð* (*habbði*, *saggði*) has been in rapid decline over the last few generations, both consonants in these clusters being pronounced as fricatives under the influence of standard spelling and the pronunciation norms of the capital, Reykjavík.[40]

As already mentioned, the development of fricatives to stops as outlined above must have begun in the thirteenth century or earlier and was largely completed in the fourteenth.

We can assume that the development *nnr* to *ðr* took place in the tenth century. In the earliest written sources and in still older poetry (to judge from the evidence of rhyme) we already find forms like *aðrir* 'other(s)', *maðr* 'man' and *suðr* 'southwards' in words where *nn* belongs to the stem

[37] Noreen 1923, 175–76.
[38] Ásgeir Bl. Magnússon 1959; Halldór Ármann Sigurðsson 1982.
[39] Noreen 1923, 40–41.
[40] Björn Guðfinnsson 1964, 144–70; Höskuldur Þráinsson and Kristján Árnason 1986, 53–60.

(cf. *annarr* '(an)other'; *mann*, acc. sg. of *maðr* 'man'; *sunnan* 'from the south'). Though the change was at first effective, analogy has often restored older *nnr* (*innri* > *iðri* > *innri* 'inner'; *finnr* > *fiðr* > *finnr* > *finnur*, third pers. sg. pres. indic. of *finna* 'to find').[41]

In the fourteenth century the pronunciation of the cluster *rl* began to merge with that of *ll*; similarly *rn* came to be pronounced in the same way as *nn* when the latter followed a long vowel or diphthong. We may assume that the result was *dl* and *dn*.[42] (It may be noted that in relatively recent loan-words and in familiar forms of personal names, e.g. *ball* 'dance' (noun), *Palli* (affectionate form of the personal name *Páll*), *ll* is not pronounced as *dl*.) While *rl* and *rn* are now pronounced *dl* and *dn*, they are also heard as *rdl* and *rdn*, particularly in words of less common occurrence. Whether this pronunciation is a survival or results from the influence of spelling is uncertain. Our understanding of the characteristic pronunciation of *rl* and *rn*, without *d*, in south-eastern Iceland suffers from the same doubt.[43]

Where *r* occurred in inflected forms of adjectives with stems ending in a vowel it was lengthened in the course of the fourteenth century (*blári* > *blárri*, dat. sg. f. of *blár* 'blue'; *hæri* > *hærri*, comp. form of *hár* 'tall'). Final *rr*, on the other hand, was shortened, first in the fourteenth century in weakly stressed endings or after a long vowel (*Einarr* > *Einar* (personal name); *stórr* > *stór* 'large'), and later after a short stressed vowel (*knörr* > *knör* 'ship' (noun)).[44] Final *ss* underwent a similar simplification (*íss*, nom. > *ís* 'ice') but it was not shortened if it belonged to the stem (as in *sess* 'seat' (noun)) or was a genitive ending (as in *íss*, gen. sg. of *ís* 'ice').[45] At the same time as *rr* and *ss* were shortened final *nn* in a weakly stressed syllable began to lose its long character, though distinction between final *nn* and *n* can still be observed in some writers down to the beginning of the eighteenth century.[46]

hv has come to be pronounced *kv* in a large part of the country. The oldest reliable evidence for the change is from the eighteenth century.[47] Where it originated is uncertain, either in the north or the west of Iceland.

---

[41] Noreen 1923, 189–90; Halldór Halldórsson 1950, 65.
[42] Alexander Jóhannesson 1923–24, 132, 135, 137; Jón Helgason 1927, 91–92; Stefán Karlsson 1993, 26–27.
[43] Björn Guðfinnsson 1964, 69–80.
[44] Björn K. Þórólfsson 1925, xxx.
[45] Björn K. Þórólfsson 1925, xxxi; Hreinn Benediktsson 1964c, 56.
[46] Björn K. Þórólfsson 1925, xxxii; Jón Helgason 1970.
[47] Gunnar Karlsson 1965; Stefán Karlsson 1967, 31.

Pronunciation of *p, t* and *k* as *b, d* and *g* is called *linmæli* 'soft speech', as opposed to *harðmæli* 'hard speech', mentioned earlier, which treats these stops as aspirates. No certain evidence of *linmæli* occurs before the latter part of the eighteenth century,[48] but it may well be older than that. *Harðmæli* is chiefly found among speakers in the east of northern Iceland and the northernmost districts of eastern Iceland.[49]

Loss of medial and final consonants (syncope and apocope) has occurred in various contexts in the spoken language but can seldom be observed in the written sources. Spelling convention and analogy with other forms where such loss did not occur meant that the written word frequently includes a consonant which would not be heard in normal speech.

Between a long vowel or diphthong and *j* fricative *g* was lost already in the thirteenth century. Later, after 1400, this *g* also disappeared between an old short vowel and a following *j* or *i* (*fleygja* 'to throw (away)' > *fleyja*; *segir* 'says' > *seiir*).[50] After *á, ó* and *ú* both *g* and *f* were lost in a final position and in a medial position when followed by *a* or *u*.[51] This loss probably began in the fifteenth century: in a document from 1447 the dat. of the farm-name *Skógar* was first written *Skofum* with the *f* subsequently corrected to *g*.[52]

Consonant loss of this kind is commonest in clusters and it has often been made an axiom that in a cluster of three the middle consonant is suppressed. This is certainly true in many cases but by no means in all. Evidence of such loss is found in the earliest written language where, for example, *morgni* (dat. sg. of *morgunn* 'morning') is invariably spelt *morni*, and *vatns* (gen. sg. of *vatn* 'water') is written without *n* (*vats, vaz*). In normal speech today the principal rule appears to be that the second consonant in a cluster tends to be lost unless it can combine with a following consonant, one or more, to form a fresh cluster. The sequence *dst*, for example, is unthinkable as an initial cluster. Consequently, while *d* is heard (as *t*) in *vindhraði* 'wind velocity', it is likely to be inaudible in *vindstig* 'wind force'; and the pres. indic. sg. of *vindast* 'to get twisted', i.e., *vin(d)st*, sounds the same as the pres. indic. sg. of *vinnast* 'to get done', i.e., *vinnst*. But the influence of the spelling and the transparent sense of a word not infrequently leads to a conscious effort to pronounce such consonants, especially when the word in question is a relatively uncommon one.

[48] Björn Guðfinnsson 1946, 234.
[49] Björn Guðfinnsson 1946, 155–243.
[50] Jón Helgason 1927, 93.
[51] Halldór Halldórsson 1950, 77; Hreinn Benediktsson 1964c, 56.
[52] *Islandske originaldiplomer* 1963, 382.

1.2.6 Parallels in related languages

Most of the sound changes described above are peculiar to Icelandic, but some are paralleled in the other Northern languages. The quantity shift, for example, took place in a broadly similar way over all Scandinavia except Denmark.[53] *hv* has become *kv* in Norwegian dialects, especially along the west coast, as well as in Faroese.[54] In some western Norwegian dialects, and in Faroese too, *rl, ll, rn* and *nn* have developed a *ddl* and *ddn* pronunciation according to rules comparable to those operative in Icelandic.[55] The characteristic Icelandic diphthongisation of *á* is also paralleled in certain western Norwegian dialects.[56] All these changes are likely to have occurred in the neighbouring countries before they were introduced in Icelandic. Indeed, it is not impossible that Norwegian pronunciation influenced Icelandic speech when relations between the two countries were at their closest in the fourteenth century. On the other hand, an obstacle in the way of postulating such influence in the case of the *hv* > *kv* change is the fact that the *kv* pronunciation is evident in Norway and the Faroes in the fourteenth century but is not apparent in Icelandic until 400 years later. Phonological developments shared by these languages are thus more likely to have been the result of latent tendencies common to all of them.

1.3 Changes of declension and conjugation

Icelandic preserves all the main features of the Old Scandinavian inflexional system. Faroese has it still to a large extent but in the other Northern languages it has been greatly simplified. Nevertheless, numerous changes of small significance have occurred in Icelandic, affecting both the inflexions of single words and sometimes whole word-classes. Some of the deviations from the ancient system have never universally prevailed, some never made headway, and some others have been suppressed. The following is no more than a concise selection among changes of this kind.

1.3.1 Nouns

Some strong declension nouns varied between classes already in the early language; nom. and acc. pl. forms (of *smiðr* 'craftsman'), *smiðar, smiða*, existed alongside *smiðir, smiði*, and the nom. and acc. pl. form (of *hǫfn* 'harbour'), *hafnar*, alongside *hafnir* (the latter forms in each case are now

---

[53] Haugen 1976, 258–60; Bandle 1973, 75–76; Kristján Árnason 1980c, 60–94.
[54] Haugen 1976, 267.
[55] Bandle 1973, 45–46.
[56] Chapman 1962, 72–73.

standard). The genitive singular of some masculine nouns varied, appearing either in -*s* or in -*ar* (e.g. *óðs, óðar*, gen. sg. of *óðr* 'poetry'). Doublets of this kind increased in number, and the genitive ending established in a personal name, e.g. *Guðmundar, Sigurðar*, may alternate in some patronymics with the other genitive ending in -*s*, *Guðmundsdóttir, Guðmundsson; Sigurðardóttir, Sigurðsson*.

A number of strong masculine nouns ended in -*ir* in the nom. pl. and in -*u* in the acc. pl. (and then often with a different stem vowel), e.g. *synir* 'sons', *sonu*. These words now have -*i* in the acc. pl. and the same stem vowel as the nominative (*synir, syni*), though in formal language and some idioms the old -*u* forms are sometimes still used (as in e.g. *koma einhverjum í opna skjöldu* 'to catch someone with his guard down', where *skjöldu* occurs in place of *skildi* as the acc. pl. of *skjöldur* 'shield'). In the Vestfirðir and Þingeyjarsýsla a nom. pl. with suffixed article, *fjörðurnar* (as opposed to *firðirnir* 'the firths'), is used, a derivation, that is, from the old acc. pl. *fjörðu*. These plural accusatives in -*u* were mostly retained until about 1500; the -*i* ending gained ground in the sixteenth century and became the virtually dominant form in the eighteenth.[57]

Many feminine nouns whose nom. sg. ended in -*r* and acc. sg. in -*i* in the old language now have the latter in the nominative as well, e.g. *heiði* 'heath', *helgi* 'weekend' (in Old Icel. 'holiday'), *veiði* 'catch' (as in fishing or hunting). This change began in the sixteenth century, but a few still keep -*r*, e.g. *brúður* 'bride' and *æður* 'eider duck', and it is retained in feminine personal names ending in e.g. -*gerður*, -*hildur*, -*gunnur*.[58]

The most notable change in noun declension occurred in masculines with -*ir* as the nom. sg. ending, *hellir* 'cave', *mælir* 'measuring device', and so on. From the fifteenth to the seventeenth century it became the norm for this ending to intrude itself between the stem and the inflexional ending in all cases except the nom. sg., first in the singular and later in the plural too. Thus the old nom. pl. *hellar* 'caves' became *hellirar* or *hellrar*. These new forms were then dominant until the nineteenth century when they lost ground as interest in and respect for the old language gathered strength and formal schooling became more widespread.[59]

Various other nouns have undergone declension changes and sometimes change of grammatical gender. Some new forms were in common use for

[57] Björn K. Þórólfsson 1925, 22–23, 84; Bandle 1956, 237–42.
[58] Björn K. Þórólfsson 1925, 81–82; Bandle 1956, 224–26.
[59] Björn K. Þórólfsson 1925, 13, 79; Bandle 1956, 204–07; Hreinn Benediktsson 1969; Kjartan G. Ottósson 1987, 314–15.

centuries but are no longer in the language, at least not as received standard. Here we can do no more than illustrate the many developments of this kind by citing a few examples.

A significant degree of confusion in *-ir* and *-ur* endings in nouns of family relationship, *bróðir* 'brother', *móðir* 'mother', *systir* 'sister', and to some extent in *faðir* 'father', is apparent already in the fifteenth century, a time when gen. sg. *föðurs* and *bróðurs* are also attested.[60]

While comparatively few masculine nouns ended in *-ur* in the plural, many feminine nouns did. This led to a tendency to treat the plural of such masculine words as if they were feminines, as indicated by forms with the suffixed article like *veturnar* (for *veturnir* 'the winters'), *bændurnar* (for *bændurnir* 'the farmers'), *eftirkomendurnar* (for *eftirkomendurnir* 'the successors'). The oldest examples of this, found already in the sixteenth century, are *fingurnar* (for *fingurnir* 'the fingers') and *fæturnar* (for *fæturnir* 'the feet') (on the model of f. pl. *hendurnar* 'the hands').[61]

Mutation and breaking could bring it about that different stem vowels occurred in different cases of the same noun. In some nouns such variation has been levelled out. The words *dyr* 'doorway' and *lykill* 'key', for example, had respectively gen. pl. *dura* and dat. sg. *lukli* in the old language, but now only forms with *y* are known. This process can be observed as early as the fourteenth century. From that time onwards *Egli* also commonly replaced *Agli* as the dat. of the personal name *Egill*, but this analogical form has now been discarded.[62]

Various nouns, weak and strong, had stems containing a *v* which remained before *a* and *i* in inflexional endings but not elsewhere. In some words in which the *v* has been retained before these endings it is now also introduced in cases with *u* endings (*söngvum, örvum*, dat. pl. of *söngur* 'song' and *ör* 'arrow' respectively; and *völvu*, oblique sg. cases of *völva* 'prophetess'). In other words the *v* has disappeared throughout the declension.[63] For example, instead of the old nom. sg. *völva* 'prophetess', oblique *völu*, we now have not only *völva* (or *valva*), oblique *völvu* (on which the neologism *tölva* 'computer' is modelled), but on the other hand *vala*, oblique *völu*, in the meaning 'knuckle-bone (used for prophecy)', where the *v*-less forms have given rise to a new nominative.[64]

[60] Björn K. Þórólfsson 1925, 29–30; Bandle 1956, 263–67.
[61] Björn K. Þórólfsson 1925, 86–87; Bandle 1956, 257–58.
[62] Finnur Jónsson 1901, 59–60; Noreen 1923, 252, 285; Björn K. Þórólfsson 1925, 4–6, 27–28; Bandle 1956, 67, 262.
[63] Björn K. Þórólfsson 1925, 10–12, 16, 26, 81; Bandle 1956, 211–14, 226.
[64] Höskuldur Þráinsson 1982; Kjartan G. Ottósson 1983 and 1987, 315–16.

A similar process is visible in nouns which had a *j* in the stem and kept it when it was followed by an *a* or *u* ending. The old words *vili* 'will' (noun) and *steði* 'anvil', for instance, have become *vilji* and *steðji* under the influence of the *j* that appears in their oblique cases. On the other hand, some other words have shed the *j* altogether: old *bryti* 'steward', oblique cases *brytja*, are now *bryti*, *bryta*.[65]

1.3.2 Adjectives and participles

Some adjectives also had *v* or *j* in the stem and these were, broadly speaking, treated in much the same way as in nouns. It is, however, only in very formal language that *v*-forms survive (*fölvan, röskvan*, acc. sg. m. of *fölur* 'pale' and *röskur* 'vigorous' respectively). *j* has also disappeared in most adjectives where it was once the norm (*ríkjan* > *ríkan, fátækjan* > *fátækan*, acc. sg. m. of *rík(u)r* 'rich', *fátæk(u)r* 'poor' respectively); an exception is *miður* 'mid(dle)', with cases like *miðjan* (acc. sg. m.) and *miðjir* (< *miðir*) (nom. pl. m.). It is also heard in a few words with *æ* or *ý* in the stem and with no consonant intervening before the inflexional ending, but in writing these are usually spelt according to the old rules, with *j* appearing before *a* and *u* but not elsewhere, as e.g. in *nýjan* but *nýir*, the acc. sg. m. and nom. pl. m. respectively of *nýr* 'new'.[66]

Before our oldest sources came to be written, *r* as an inflexional adjectival element was assimilated to a preceding *s* and produced a long consonant, *ss*. This occurred in the nom. sg. m. (*lauss* 'loose', 'free'), in the dat. and gen. sg. f. and the gen. pl. of all genders: compare those cases of *góðr* 'good', i.e., *góðri, góðrar, góðra*, with the corresponding ones of *lauss*, i.e., *laussi, laussar, laussa*. In certain circumstances this *r* was also assimilated to a preceding *l* or *n*, i.e., where an adjective ends in *-ll* or *-nn* in the nom. sg. m.; here the dat. sg. f., for example, also had the same double consonant (*gamall* 'old', *gamalli*; *beinn* 'straight', *beinni*). Analogy with the forms of most adjectives led to the reintroduction of *r* in these endings, already by about 1300 in the adjectives in *-s* (*lausri*), and in these it became the standard form. In the sixteenth century and later *r* reappeared in the words in *-ll* and *-nn* (*gamallri, hreinnri*). These forms were dominant in the eighteenth century but they have since fallen out of use and for the most part the old forms have been reinstated.[67]

---

[65] Björn K. Þórólfsson 1925, 24–25; Halldór Halldórsson 1950, 103–04.
[66] Björn K. Þórólfsson 1925, 34–35, 89–90; Bandle 1956, 308–11.
[67] Noreen 1923, 200; Björn K. Þórólfsson 1925, 33, 88; Bandle 1956, 297–300; Kjartan G. Ottósson 1987, 316–17.

In the old language the derivative suffixes, -*ag*-, -*ig*- and -*ug*-, used in the formation of adjectives, lost their vowel when the following inflexional ending began with a vowel (e.g. m. sg. *gǫfugr* 'noble', pl. *gǫfgir*). Around 1300 the force of analogy began to bring about a restoration of the syncopated vowel (*göfgir* > *göfugir*), a development which gradually became general. On the other hand, the adj. *heilagr* 'holy' was treated in such a way as to make the uncontracted/contracted alternation (*heilagur, helgan*) redundant. It was split between two distinct declensions (*heilagur, heilagir; helgur, helgir*).[68]

The past participle of a strong verb was declined like the adjectival class represented e.g. by *opinn* 'open'; the past participle of a weak verb followed the commonest adjectival pattern, i.e., with acc. sg. m. in -*an* (*kallaðr, kallaðan*, pp. of *kalla* 'to call'). Past participle forms have undergone some change over the centuries, particularly in verbs conjugated like *berja* 'to beat', *barði*. These originally had *ð* in all cases of the participle (though in contracted forms the *ð* might appear as *d* or *t* in certain clusters, cf. § 1.2.5 above), and *ið* if the inflexional ending did not begin with a vowel: thus m. sg. *bariðr* 'beaten', *barðan, bariðs, bǫrðum*. But we find already in the oldest texts that verbs of this class with a stem ending in a dental, and a few other verbs as well, have contracted past participle forms, e.g. *hvattr, kvaddr, spurðr*, nom. sg. m. pp. of *hvetja* 'to encourage', *kveðja* 'to bid farewell', and *spyrja* 'to inquire of' respectively. Around 1200 similar contraction becomes apparent in the past participles of more verbs, especially in the nom. sg. (e.g. *barðr* 'beaten'). This development was, however, confined to a small group of past participles (e.g. *lagðr*, nom. sg. m. pp. of *leggja* 'to place') and did not lead to wholesale change. On the other hand, around 1300 the past participles of strong verbs in -*in(n)* began to influence the uncontracted forms of their counterparts in the *berja* class. We find nom. sg. m. *barinn* 'beaten' replacing *bariðr*, and later in use for acc. sg. m. as well, *barinn* for *barðan*. The contracted forms that lost the *i* of *ið* before a vowel ending remained unaffected, and this gave rise to the characteristic mixed forms of most of these participial adjectives. The past participle of *berja*, for example, is now declined in the m. sg. *barinn, barinn, barins, börðum*.[69]

The forms of positive and superlative adjectives when declined weak were essentially the same as they are today. An exception is that between

---

[68] Björn K. Þórólfsson 1925, 31–32; Bandle 1956, 300–02.
[69] Björn K. Þórólfsson 1925, 62–63, 116–17; Bandle 1956, 408–11; Jón Hilmar Jónsson 1979.

about 1600 and 1800 the dat. pl. ending, originally -*um* (*enum spǫkustum mǫnnum* '(for) the wisest people'), was gradually discarded in favour of -*u* (the ending of the other plural cases).[70] Comparative adjectives and present participles underwent the same change in the dat. pl., but were also subject to a number of further modifications. The oblique m. sg. cases once ended in *a* (e.g. acc. *spakara mann* 'a wiser person', *spyrjanda lærisvein* 'an inquiring disciple'), but this was replaced by *i*. In the n. sg. the *a*-ending was retained in a comparative adjective (*spakara barn* 'a wiser child') but it was replaced by *i* in the n. sg. of a present participle used adjectivally (*spyrjanda barn* > *spyrjandi barn* 'an inquiring child'). This means that the present participle now has the -*i* ending throughout the paradigm.[71]

1.3.3 Pronouns

The pronominal stock of Modern Icelandic differs most sharply from that of the old language in that it has abandoned the dual number that existed in the first and second person pronouns and their concomitant possessive adjectives. There are now only singular and plural forms, as in other words distinguished by number. The old dual forms were *vit* 'we two' and *(þ)it* 'you two' with poss. adjs. *okkarr, ykkarr* '(belonging to the two of us', 'belonging to the two of you' respectively). Plural forms, which could also be used in an honorific sense of a single person, were *vér* 'we' and *(þ)ér* 'you', with poss. adjs. *várr* 'our' (later *vor*) and *yð(v)arr* 'your'. Occasional deviations from this distinct usage may be observed in early texts but for the most part the usage of these forms did not change until the seventeenth century and in some localities not before the eighteenth. Since then, however, the old dual forms have been virtually dominant, used in almost any context where more than one person is referred to, the Bible being the one exception. The old plural forms also remain but are largely confined to formal contexts, *vér*, for example, used by someone in public office, and *þér* as an honorific form of address to a single person.[72]

The old possessive adjectives, *okkarr, ykkarr, yðvarr*, were replaced by the gen. of the corresponding personal pronoun. This simplification was largely completed in the sixteenth century.[73]

In the early language the demonstrative pronoun, 'this', 'that', had the form *sjá* in the nom. sg. m. and f. This lived on until late in the fourteenth

[70] Björn K. Þórólfsson 1925, 90–91; Bandle 1956, 311–13.
[71] Björn K. Þórólfsson 1925, 36–37, 91–93; Bandle 1956, 320–23.
[72] Björn K. Þórólfsson 1925, 41–42, 97, 101; Bandle 1956, 347–51; Helgi Guðmundsson 1972.
[73] Björn K. Þórólfsson 1925, 45, 99–100; Bandle 1956, 349–51.

century when it was generally superseded by *þessi*. The acc. sg. m. was *þenna* but in the fifteenth century it was more and more often replaced by *þennan*. At an early stage the stem *þess-* was augmented by *-ar(-)* in the gen. and dat. sg. f. and the gen. pl. (*þessi, þessar, þessa* > *þessari, þessarar, þessara*). Such forms were already common in the fourteenth century.[74]

Various other pronouns have undergone changes from Old to Modern Icelandic, not least *nokkur, nokkuð* 'some(one/thing)', 'any(one/thing)'. In the oldest Icelandic this most often appeared as *nekkverr* or *nakkvarr* in the nom. sg. m., with corresponding adjectival endings in the plural and the oblique cases. By the second half of the thirteenth century these forms were generally superseded by *nökkurr* and *nokkurr* and in the following centuries the latter form in *-o-* became dominant. The second syllable *-ur* was at first retained in all the inflected forms but the *-u-* came to be dropped in the fifteenth century whenever the inflexional ending began with a vowel (*nokkurum* > *nokkrum*).[75]

1.3.4 Verbs

Verb forms have experienced various changes, particularly some strong verbs, a few of which have come to be conjugated weak, either completely or in part. Examples with their old preterites in parenthesis are *ríta*, now *rita*, 'to write' (*reit*), *hrinda* 'to push' (*hratt*), *bjarga* 'to save' (*barg*), *hjálpa* 'to help' (*halp*), *fregna* 'to learn of' (*frá*), *þvá*, later *þvo*, 'to wash' (*þó*). Nevertheless, the past participle *þveginn* 'washed' remains as a relic of the strong conjugation of *þvá*, as do *borginn* (as in *einhverjum er borgið* 'someone is safe and sound') and *hólpinn* ('safe', 'secure'), old past participles of *bjarga* and *hjálpa*. The weak form *séður* 'seen' has replaced older *sénn* as the past participle of *sjá* ' to see'. Most of these strong verbs had adopted their weak forms by about the middle of the sixteenth century.[76]

Various analogical changes have taken place in verbal endings. About 1300, third person singular forms were replacing first person forms (this did not apply, of course, where the two forms were already identical, *ek fór* 'I went', *hann fór* 'he went'). Thus in the preterite indicative, *ek sagða* 'I said', for example, became *eg sagði*; in the present subjunctive *ek segja* 'I (may) say' became *eg segi*; in the preterite subjunctive *ek segða* 'I would say' became *eg segði*. In the following centuries new forms of this kind made inroads, not all at the same pace, and they may be said to have

---

[74] Björn K. Þórólfsson 1925, 46–47; Bandle 1956, 352–53.
[75] Björn K. Þórólfsson 1925, 49–50, 106; Bandle 1956, 368–69; Hreinn Benediktsson 1961–62a.
[76] Bandle 1956, 395–406; Kjartan G. Ottósson 1987, 318–20.

carried the day in the seventeenth century. Early in the fourteenth century the same tendency can be observed in the present indicative singular as well, with *eg segir* for older *ek segi* 'I say', for example. This usage is attested down to the sixteenth century, when the old forms were re-established and were soon in almost universal use. The chief exception was in the verb 'to be', *vera*, whose old first person singular present indicative form, *em* 'am', was gradually ousted by *er*.

Influence of indicative forms also led to changes in those of the subjunctive plural. This applied to the first person plural of the present tense, where older subjunctive *segim* '(we) (may) say' became *segjum*, for example, and to all persons of the preterite plural, where older *segðim, segðið, segði* 'we, you (pl.), they would say' became *segðum, segðuð, segðu* respectively.

In Old Icelandic the second person singular of the preterite indicative of a strong verb ended in *t* (e.g. *þú fórt*, inf. *fara* 'to go'), or (usually) in *tt* if the verb stem ended in a vowel (e.g. *þú bjótt*, inf. *búa* 'to dwell'). If, however, the verbal stem ended in a *t* the second person ending was *st*, more often appearing as *zt* (*þú brauzt*, inf. *brjóta* 'to break', *þú ba(t)zt*, inf. *binda* 'to bind'). *st*-endings also naturally occurred in the second singular preterite of verbs ending in *s* (*þú blést*, inf. *blása* 'to blow') and in all the singular preterite forms of verbs ending in *-st* (*ek, þú, hann laust*, inf. *ljósta* 'to strike'). These pervading forms in *-st* came to exert a wider influence with the result that in the first half of the sixteenth century we begin to detect *-st* as the ending of the second person singular preterite of other strong verbs than those just listed. This *-st* usage became altogether regular in the seventeenth century.

When epenthetic *u* entered the language (see § 1.2.3 above), the second person singular of the present indicative of most strong verbs came to end in *-ur* (*þú kemur* < *þú kemr*, inf. *koma* 'to come'). If the stem of a strong verb ended in *r* or *s*, on the other hand, the second person singular form remained monosyllabic (*þú ferr* > *þú fer*, inf. *fara* 'to go'; *þú less* > *þú les*, inf. *lesa* 'to read'). In the eighteenth century we can observe the addition of a final *ð* or *t* to these forms, under the influence of suffixed forms of the pronoun: *þú ferð* 'you (sg.) go', cf. *ferðu* < *fer þú*; *þú lest* 'you (sg.) read', cf. *lestu* < *les þú*).[77]

Some larger changes have affected middle voice endings. Around 1200 the first person singular ended in *-umk* (*ek kǫllumk* 'I am called'), where

---

[77] Jón Þorkelsson 1887 and 1888–94; Björn K. Þórólfsson 1925, 53–66, 108–20; Bandle 1956, 377–427; Orešnik 1980.

the *mk* was derived from the accusative of the first person pronoun, *mik* 'me'. The other personal forms ended in *-sk* (< *sik*) or *-zk*, and it was this latter form (irrespective of whether it was preceded by a dental or not) which gradually gained ground. The *-sk* or *-zk* ending was introduced into the first person already about 1200 (*ek kǫllumsk*), and soon afterwards the mutated form of the stem began to be abandoned (*ek kallask*). In the course of the thirteenth century the *-sk/-zk* endings were gradually replaced by *-z* alone, which early fourteenth-century manuscripts show to have been then the dominant form. This *-z* ending lived on until after 1400 but met increasing competition from forms in *-zt* and *-zst* that arose later in the fourteenth century. In the fifteenth century *-zt* became the dominant form. Alongside *-zt* a form in *-st* sometimes appeared, particularly after *l* and *r* (*dvelst*, third pers. sg. pres. indic. of *dveljast* 'to stay'; *berst*, third pers. sg. pres. indic. of *berast* 'be carried' or of *berjast* 'to fight'), but this normal modern ending did not become common before the sixteenth century, after *z* had lost its independent phonetic value (cf. p. 19 above). What that value had been in the early middle voice endings just discussed has been a matter for debate. The facts given above would suggest that the changes in the first person plural from about 1200 to 1400 went along these lines: *berjumsk* > *berjumzk* > *berjumz* > *berjumzt* 'we('ll) fight'. After 1400 new forms appear, at first with endings *-nzt* and *-zt* and later *-nst* and *-st* (*berjunst, berjust*). These forms were more or less dominant in the sixteenth and the seventeenth century. After 1600 yet another ending made its appearance with the addition of *-um* to the *-st* ending (*berjustum*), and this gradually became widespread. But in the eighteenth century scholars began to revive an older ending in the form *-umst*. After 1800 this form gained ground and became the standard form in the written language, but in speech *-ustum* is still common.[78]

1.4 Lexicon

The vocabulary of early Icelandic was almost entirely Scandinavian, with just a few Celtic loan-words brought in by the first settlers, as indicated above (§ 1.1.3). In this same early period a number of more exotic loan-words arrived, acquired by Vikings and other adventurers, some of them members of the Varangian Guard in Byzantium: *torg* 'market' came from Slavonic, for example,[79] and *fíll* 'elephant' ultimately from Persian.[80]

---

[78] Noreen 1923, 367–73; Björn K. Þórólfsson 1925, 67–71, 120–21; Bandle 1956, 175–77, 393–95; Kjartan G. Ottósson 1987, 315, and 1992.

[79] de Vries 1962, xxxiii and 595.

[80] Fischer 1909, 44.

1.4.1 The language of the Church

Christian missions, the conversion to Christianity, and the whole apparatus of the Church naturally augmented the vocabulary of Icelandic in many spheres and at an early stage. This is amply demonstrated by the oldest ecclesiastical literature we possess, a good deal of it from the twelfth century. A number of words of Latin origin (some originally from Greek) belong here, many of them introduced by way of other Germanic languages. They include, for example, *engill* 'angel', *biskup* 'bishop', *prestr* 'priest', *djákni* 'deacon', *kirkja* 'church', *klaustr* 'cloister', 'convent', *altari* 'altar' and *obláta* 'sacramental wafer'.[81] Old Saxon and Old English were substantial donors: *synd* 'sin' came from the former,[82] *þolinmóðr*, *þolinmæði* 'long-suffering' (adj. and noun respectively) from the latter.[83] The word *guðspjall* 'gospel' itself is from Old English *godspell* 'good tidings', a translation of Latin *evangelium* 'message of joy'.[84]

In its earliest stages the ecclesiastical language was for the most part based upon Scandinavian stems. The Icelanders soon showed independence and resilience in their response to the challenge of finding native expressions for the many novelties of thought and action introduced in their new Christian world.[85] Words already in the language were given a specialised Christian sense, and further terms were derived from them. As an example may be taken the verb *freista*, of whose two main senses, 'to try' and 'to tempt', the former appears to have been the original one. The derivative noun *freistni* 'temptation', in any case, almost certainly originated in Church language.[86]

We cannot always be sure whether such neologisms were first created in Norway or Iceland, since it is seldom possible to tell in which country the oldest extant religious literature—homilies and saints' lives—was first composed or translated. The communities speaking West Scandinavian maintained so substantial a uniformity of language (cf. § 1.1.3 above) that down to the fourteenth century they constituted a single reading public. The word *samviska* 'conscience', for instance, is a literal translation of the Latin compound *conscientia*, and it was probably invented in thirteenth-century Norway. Before that, 'conscience' was variously rendered by

---

[81] Jakob Benediktsson 1964, 95–96.
[82] Halldór Halldórsson 1968 and 1969.
[83] Walter 1976b, 82–83.
[84] de Vries 1962, 193.
[85] Jón Helgason 1958, 16; Stefán Karlsson 1985.
[86] Walter 1976b, 92–93.

words meaning, *inter alia*, 'thought', 'mind', 'understanding': *hugr, hugvit, hugskot*; but once in being *samviska* became the established term.[87]

1.4.2 Other foreign influences

As Icelanders in time became acquainted with European chivalric culture, partly through romances translated from French or Anglo-Norman in both Norway and Iceland, a number of new words entered the language. The best-known of these are doubtless the key-words, *kurteiss* 'courteous', 'courtly', and *kurteisi* 'courtesy', 'chivalry'. New words for new objects and commodities, terms like *silki* 'silk', *skarlat* 'scarlet (cloth)', *klaret* 'spiced wine', *pansari* 'coat of mail', *organ* '(church) organ', came in both through this literature and through commerce.[88]

Trade and the presence of North Germans in Denmark, Sweden and Norway, especially in the townships, meant that the late Middle Ages saw a vast influx of Low German words into the Scandinavian languages. German merchants did not begin to sail to Iceland until the late fourteenth century, but German loan-words probably came first and largely into Icelandic by indirect routes. At first both German and Danish vocabulary came by way of Norwegian; later there was direct Danish influence and with it many Danish loans from German. Documents from the late fifteenth century and on into the sixteenth show more and more vocabulary from these foreign sources. Examples with their modern German and Danish equivalents in parentheses are *blífa* 'to stay', 'remain' (*bleiben, blive*); *þenkja* 'to think' (*denken, tænke*); *bífala* 'to command' (*befehlen, befale*); *makt* 'power' (*Macht, magt*); *selskapur* 'group of people met together' (*Gesellschaft, selskab*).[89] Many of the oldest loan-words of ultimate German origin were adopted to express concepts for which words already existed in Icelandic and were thus in competition with synonyms or near-synonyms of native growth.

1.4.3 The Reformation

Printed books in Low German and Danish were reaching Iceland in the years around 1500 and were in some cases translated. The influence of the ideas of the German and Danish divines who were active in seeking Church reform began to be felt in Iceland in the 1530s and the Reformation was fully effected there in 1550. The new dispensation encouraged trans-

---

[87] Widding 1961; Halldór Halldórsson 1964a, 110.
[88] Jakob Benediktsson 1964, 96–98.
[89] Westergård-Nielsen 1946; Veturliði Óskarsson 2003.

lation on a grand scale, almost all from Danish and German, whether the books in question were original in these languages or were themselves translations, and it was now counted of prime importance to disseminate the translated works in print. Accustomed as they were to manuscript books in their native tongue, the Icelandic advocates of the Reformation found it entirely natural to make these writings available to their countrymen in their own language. In this they differed from their kinsmen in Norway and the Faroes whose Bible and other works of religious edification came to them in Danish. A translation of the New Testament, put into Icelandic by Oddur Gottskálksson (died 1556), was printed in 1540, and the whole Bible, edited by Bishop Guðbrandur Þorláksson (1542–1627), appeared in 1584. Behind these translations lay the medieval Icelandic tradition of Christian literature, which often solved the Reformers' translation problems for them, but these works and others from foreign sources, hymns and sermons for example, contained many loan-words, some already established in the language, others more recently current or quite new.[90] A good many of these imported words had the prefixes *bí-* (later more often *be-*) and *for-*, e.g. *bíhaga* 'to please', 'to suit', *bíkvæmilegur* 'pleasant', 'comfortable', *fordjarfa* 'to spoil', 'to damage', *fornema* 'to understand'. While it is doubtful whether many of the rarer and more abstract loan-words were adopted in popular usage, German and Danish influence on both the vocabulary and the syntax of writing in the service of the Church in Iceland remained strong until the nineteenth century. Then a more natural native idiom was restored, not least by the Icelandic Bible Society's New Testament, published in 1827, and its whole Bible, published in 1841.[91]

1.4.4 Other Danish influences

Since from about the time of the Reformation until well into the nineteenth century, Iceland's foreign relations were amost exclusively with Denmark, the influence of Danish in more spheres than that of the Church may well be expected. Not only was the administration of Icelandic affairs centered in Copenhagen; the governor of Iceland was usually a high-ranking Dane or Norwegian. Local officials had to conduct all business with their superiors in Danish and all government edicts were promulgated in Danish. This latter arrangement was modified about 1750 when such announce-

---

[90] Jón Helgason 1929 and 1931, 36–42; Westergård-Nielsen 1946; Bandle 1956, 269–84, 317–20, 427–30; Árni Böðvarsson 1964, 184–87; Jakob Benediktsson 1964, 100–02; Stefán Karlsson 1984.

[91] Jón Helgason 1931, 49; Steingrímur J. Þorsteinsson 1950.

ments began to be accompanied by an Icelandic text, but was not abolished until a century or so later. The inevitable result was that the Icelandic written by civil servants was generally saturated with Danicisms.[92]

Icelandic commerce long remained a Danish monopoly and this also exerted a strong influence on the native language. Danish terms for commodities were naturally adopted but in time the advent of Danish merchants had profounder effects. The small trading stations which were established in the eighteenth century grew into communities where the population was partly Danish. A famous opinion, voiced by the great Danish philologist, Rasmus Rask (1787–1832), shortly after his arrival in Reykjavík in 1813, was that within a century nobody in the township would understand Icelandic, and that within two hundred years nobody in the country would understand it unless, as he said, 'drastic measures are taken'.[93]

1.4.5 The native inheritance

The language of some social groups, or at least their written language, thus became very much intermingled with Danish, but everyday speech and the stories and poems of the people at large kept alive the greater part of the native lexicon. Farming was the principal occupation and its techniques changed little over the centuries. People went on talking about much the same things in the course of their daily toil and, although much printed matter was affected by Danish, printed matter was by no means the only resource available for private reading or for reading aloud to a group. Medieval Icelandic literature maintained its vital hold, even though little of it was accessible in print before the nineteenth century. The early saints' lives were probably not much read after the Reformation, but sagas of Icelanders, kings' sagas, and not least the sagas of antiquity (*fornaldarsögur*) and romances (*riddarasögur*), were read in old manuscripts and innumerable copies of them made. The old poetic diction lived on in the rhymed narrative poems called *rímur*, some of them medieval in origin and many others made by later versifiers; and to some extent poetry of other kinds maintained the same tradition. Snorri Sturluson's *Edda* remained a guide for poets. It is extant in many copies, and the version made by Magnús Ólafsson of Laufás (1573–1636) was especially popular, even before it was printed in Copenhagen in 1665.[94] Neither should we forget *Jónsbók*, the Icelanders' law-code introduced in 1281. From about

---

[92] Jón Helgason 1931, 42–44.
[93] Jakob Benediktsson 1964, 104.
[94] *Two Versions of Snorra Edda*, 1977–79.

1300 to 1700 more manuscript copies of this work are known than of any other Icelandic text—in addition, a printed edition appeared in Iceland in 1580 and another in the eighteenth century. The many manuscripts and various scrawls found in their margins show that *Jónsbók* was partly used as a first reading primer. Boys in better-off homes were evidently made to read it over and over, learning to read but also learning the law in its ancient wording.

1.4.6 Purism and conscious cultivation of the language

A Latin description of Iceland, written about 1589 and attributed to Bishop Oddur Einarsson (1559–1630), remarks that the ancient literature of Iceland is written in a language which was once the common language of the Scandinavian peoples and adds that this native language of the Icelanders has remained unspoilt down to the present day.[95] Arngrímur Jónsson, 'the learned', made much the same observation in a Latin work, *Crymogæa*, first published in 1609.[96] He attributed the preservation of the language to the existence and circulation of old manuscripts and to his country's geographical isolation. He warned his countrymen against German and Danish influence on their Icelandic, whether spoken or written. Texts published or revised by Arngrímur show that he reduced the number of loan-words in them and amended their syntax to more natural Icelandic patterns.[97]

Relatively pure Icelandic, with sparing use of loan-words, is found in a number of other writers of both prose and poetry in the seventeenth and early eighteenth century. The great poet, Hallgrímur Pétursson (*c.*1614–1674), and the great preacher, Bishop Jón Vídalín (1666–1720), are prime examples; but there were others too who prized carefully written Icelandic. It was only later in the eighteenth century, however, that a purist policy came to be clearly proclaimed, urging, *inter alia*, the purposeful coining of new words on the basis of native stems. In that century Icelandic came to be employed in the translation and composition of works on a variety of subjects which had never, or hardly ever, been treated in Icelandic before. Neologisms were inevitable, many of them loan-translations from other languages. Jón Ólafsson from Grunnavík (1705–1779), secretary to Árni Magnússon (died 1730) and later stipendiary of the Arnamagnæan Foun-

---

[95] Oddur Einarsson 1971, 81, 145.
[96] Arngrímur Jónsson 1950–57, II 25–30 and IV 285–86.
[97] Jón Helgason 1931, 39, 41; Jakob Benediktsson 1953; Árni Böðvarsson 1964, 187–88.

dation in Copenhagen,[98] was typically active in the field but since hardly any of his translations or his own writings in Icelandic were published, his views and his neologisms were little known to his contemporaries. It was, however, in his lifetime that the Danes themselves became interested in purism and the programmatic cultivation of their native language. In Iceland it was the efforts of Eggert Ólafsson (1726–1768) that made a greater impact than Jón Ólafsson's work. After Eggert's death, the publications of Lærdómslistafélag, the 'Learned Arts Society', founded in 1779, were especially influential. In the spirit of the Enlightenment it produced a series of publications between 1781 and 1798 with papers treating a very wide range of subjects.[99] Linguistic purity was part of the Society's programme, and the novel topics called for the creation of many new words. Some purists of the time were found to go too far in adopting archaic diction. Magnús Stephensen (1762–1833) praised the fine Icelandic of Bishop Jón Vídalín and Bishop Hannes Finnsson (1739–1796), but he went on to say that their writings must surely strike all good men as 'more accessible and expressive than the unattractive archaic doggerel heard even in prose, and the botched imagery produced by a few poetasters imitating the obscurity of ancient verse'.[100]

There was some change in attitudes towards the cultivation of Icelandic in the first half of the nineteenth century. Those most concerned were Sveinbjörn Egilsson (1791–1852), headmaster of the Bessastaðir grammar school, colleagues of his and later their pupils, Baldvin Einarsson (1801–1833) and the group associated with the periodical *Fjölnir*. Of particular note among them were Konráð Gíslason (1808–1891), who became professor of Nordic philology in the University of Copenhagen, and the poet Jónas Hallgrímsson (1807–1845).[101] These men were affected by the Romantic Movement and it was clear to them that good Icelandic was to be found not only in old books but also on the lips of the people. Even though some of their predecessors in favour of purism had taken pains to use words, old or new, of native origin, the structure of their sentences often betrayed the influence of the official or learned style of Danish and German. Writing in a fresh and relatively supple style, much closer to the spoken language

---

[98] Jón Helgason 1926a, 36–37, 66–67, 74–76, 120.
[99] Vilhjálmur Þ. Gíslason 1923, 276–94; Jón Helgason 1931, 45–48, and 1954, 98–99; Árni Böðvarsson 1964, 188–96; Halldór Halldórsson 1964b, 137–41; Jakob Benediktsson 1964, 104–05; Halldór Halldórsson 1971, 222–25.
[100] Magnús Stephensen 1806, 523.
[101] Bjarni Vilhjálmsson 1944.

than before, the editors of *Fjölnir* and their allies took it upon themselves to lay a new foundation for the written language of the Icelanders.[102]

It may be said that essentially the same policy has been followed ever since. It is true that many foreign words have entered the language and some of them have adapted well to the phonetic and inflexional system of Icelandic, but the main tendency has been to form new words from native stems. At the same time the many loan-words which were commonplace two centuries ago have gradually been replaced by native words, both ancient and modern. The language of the most recent generations is not considered here in any detail, but the change has undoubtedly been much greater in the written language than in the spoken, for many Icelanders who use foreign words freely in speech try hard to avoid them when writing matter intended for publication. It is worth noting, however, that a good many of the thousands of new words that have been invented have been short-lived. It has not always been possible for a neologism to replace a loan-word, at least not in the spoken language (*bíll* 'car', from Danish *bil, automobil*, has not given way to *bifreið*, for instance; *vindill* 'cigar' from *vinda* 'to wind, roll' is a standard word, but the diminutive *vindlingur* 'cigarette' belongs only to the official written language, while *sígaretta* is used in speech). No less frequently, in contrast, more than one neologism has been proposed for the same thing, with only one emerging victorious from the competition: 'concept' is *hugtak*, not its older equivalent *hugargrip*; 'the present' is *nútíð*, not *nástund*; the 'divide-sign' in arithmetic is *deilingarmerki*, not *deildarnóti*.[103]

---

[102] Vilhjálmur Þ. Gíslason 1923, 294–304; Jón Helgason 1931, 48–50; Björn Guðfinnsson 1941; Nanna Ólafsdóttir 1961, 165–70; Árni Böðvarsson 1964, 197–99; Halldór Halldórsson 1964b, 141–42; Jakob Benediktsson 1964, 105–06; Halldór Halldórsson 1971, 225–26.

[103] Jón Helgason 1954; Halldór Halldórsson 1971; Baldur Jónsson 1976; Kjartan G. Ottósson 1990.

---

(1) From a church dedication day homily, twelfth century. AM 237 a fol., fol. 1ra.

Hurþ fyr duru*m* merker scynsama me*n*n. þa es hraústlega standa at móte villo mænno*m*. oc byrgia þa fyr utan c*r*istne goþs í kenningo*m* síno*m*. Gólf þile kirkio merker litillata me*n*n. þa es sic lǽgia í allre virþíngo. oc veíta þvi meira upp halld ællo*m* lyþ. se*m* þeír verþa meirr. under foto*m* troþner. Seto pallar kir*kio* merk*er*. varcunnlata me*n*n. þa es heógia meíno*m* o styrcra nǫ́nga í var cunnlǽte síno. sua se*m* pallar veíta hogynde sitiondo*m*.

2. Orthography

2.1 The first attempts

The homicide section, *Vígslóði*, and some other parts of the early Icelandic laws were recorded in writing in the winter 1117–1118. This would hardly have been undertaken if writing the vernacular on vellum was not to some extent already practised.

The first writers of Icelandic undoubtedly learnt to read and write from Latin books. Archaic traces in the oldest manuscripts have led to the conclusion that it was the roman alphabet which from the start was used as far as possible for giving Icelandic a written form. The sound systems of Latin and Icelandic were, however, very different. As noted earlier (§ 1.2.1), the earliest Icelandic had nine different vowels (ignoring vowel-length and nasality), while there were only five vowel-signs in the roman alphabet, *a, e, i, o* and *u*. For want of more symbols, the Icelanders were compelled to use *e* for the two sounds, *e* and *é*; *o* for *o* and *ø* and probably for *ǫ*; *u* and its variant, *v*, for both *u* and *y*. The diphthongs *ei* and *au* could be written as they are now, but *au/av* also served as the symbol for *ey*.[104] There are moreover indications in the oldest manuscripts that Icelandic diphthongs were written with monophthong symbols, a fact which possibly shows that the Icelanders were acquainted with North German and East Scandinavian vernacular writings. The Icelandic Church first belonged to the archdiocese of Hamburg–Bremen, from 1056 to 1104, and then to the archdiocese of Lund, from 1104 to 1152/53, and these metropolitan sees were both in speech-areas where the equivalent old diphthongs had been monophthongised.[105]

The earliest extant manuscripts, probably written about 1150 and later, show that various attempts were made to differentiate regular vowels and their mutated forms. Some of the symbols used had foreign models, not least English. The letter *y*, for example, most probably came from English,

[104] Hreinn Benediktsson 1965, 29–30, 56–57.
[105] Stefán Karlsson 1977, 129–30.

The door before the portal signifies people of good sense, who stand firm against heretics and exclude them from the Church of God in their teachings. The wooden floor of the church signifies the humble, who place themselves low in every kind of estimation, and who give all the more support to everyone, the more they are trodden underfoot. The church pews signify the merciful, who, in their mercy, lessen the misfortunes of their weak neighbours, just as pews give comfort to those sitting in them.

and it rapidly established itself as the normal sign for this vowel in Icelandic. Various symbols were adopted for mutated vowels: digraphs (two free-standing characters), ligatures (two characters joined together), and marked characters, i.e., letters marked by a stroke or hook. After short *e* and short *ę* fell together, the sound expressed as *ę* (see § 1.2.1 above) existed only as a long vowel, and for this the digraph *ae* was used only exceptionally, while *æ* and *ę* predominated. For *ø* the digraph *eo* was common in the oldest manuscripts, though *ø* is also found. The digraph *ao* for *ǫ* is rare; ligatured *a+o (ǫ)* and *ǫ* are the more usual forms.[106]

The consonant symbols of the roman alphabet were on the whole adequate for Icelandic purposes. A chief lack was a symbol for *þ* (or *ð*). This sound, unvoiced or voiced, is sometimes, but rarely, represented by *th* in the oldest sources, but *þ* is by far the most usual symbol for it. Icelanders must have been familiar with *þ* from the runic alphabet, but they probably introduced it into their script from Old English. They called the letter *þorn*, which is the English name for it (and which means 'thorn', both in Old English and in Old Norse); in the Scandinavian runic alphabets it is called *þurs* (meaning 'giant').[107]

The author of the First Grammatical Treatise,[108] writing about the middle of the twelfth century, set himself the task of bringing order into Icelandic orthography. His basic aim was to make do with as few different characters as possible while at the same time retaining enough to ensure that no disagreement could arise over the way the written word was to be read. He chose to represent the four mutation vowels by *ę, y, ø* and *ǫ*; and he wished to make clear the distinction between long and short vowels by placing an accent over the long sounds or a dot if the sound was both long and nasal.

The author of the Treatise added *þ* to the inventory of the roman alphabet, but he also found some roman letters superfluous. He recommended the

[106] Hreinn Benediktsson 1965, 24–30, 45, 56–59.
[107] Hreinn Benediktsson 1965, 21–22.
[108] *Islands grammatiske litteratur* I 1886; Holtsmark 1936; Haugen 1950; Hreinn Benediktsson 1972.

---

(2) From *Veraldarsaga*, c.1200. AM 655 VIII 4to, fol. 2v.

Ana/þ su es gv́þingar hǫ́fþo á egípta lande. af pharaó konunge. merker þrældo*m* þan es diofǫ́ll þrǽlcar allt mankv́ɴ í heíþno*m*dome. oc lausn su es gvþ leídde þa uɴdaɴ anauþeɴe mérker frǽlse þat es gvþ géfr sino*m* móno*m* þa es þeir krístnasc. Siǫr eɴ rauþe sa es þeir gengo igegno*m* m*er*ker skirnar bruɴeɴ. þaɴ es helgaþr es af bana bloþe c*r*ists. Pharao oc heʀ ha*n*s sa es drucnaþi i sioeno*m* rauþa. ᴍ*er*ker fiandaɴ. oc svnþ*er* er af hverio*m* maɴe deyia ískirnar vatne.

letter *c* for short *k*, dismissing *k* and *q* as alternatives. He counted *x* and *z* as unnecessary since they each stood for two sounds (cf. § 1.2.5 above) and could be equally well written *cs* and *ds*. He proposed representing long (double) consonants by small capital letters (i.e., with the form of roman capitals but of no greater height than ordinary lower-case letters). His one exception here was long *k* (*kk*), for which he advocated a special form of *k*, derived from the Greek alphabet. (Cf. extracts 1 and 2.)

2.2 The thirteenth and fourteenth centuries

It may as well be said at once that no manuscript is preserved in which the spelling rules of the First Grammatical Treatise are followed with any sort of consistency. Most thirteenth-century scribes show the influence of some of the author's recommendations, however, and traces of them are still to be found in the fourteenth century.

Sound changes during this period, *c.*1200–1400, rendered some of the First Grammarian's rules redundant. There is, for example, no trace of any distinction made in writing between nasal and oral vowels. (On this point see now, however, footnote 165 below.) As mentioned above, the oldest manuscripts vary greatly in their representation of mutated vowels, and this variety increased when the short vowels ø and ǫ fell together and the long vowels ę́ and ǿ did the same. In the normalised spelling familiar to many from the editions of the *Íslenzk fornrit* series these last-mentioned sounds are represented by æ and œ (ligatured o+e), and these symbols will be used in what follows for the vowel sounds in question. *ONP* uses the signs ǽ and ǿ.

The commonest symbols for ø were *eo, ø, o* and *ey*; for ǫ they were ǫ, ǫ, *a*' and *o*. After ø and ǫ fell together, the chief symbols for the resulting vowel sound were ø, ǫ, *o* and *a*', though *au/av* were also used. Of these ø is comparatively rare, and in the fourteenth century the form ǫ was gradually superseded by ǫ́. The vowel sound that resulted from the falling together of ø and *o* is here represented by ö, as in Modern Icelandic, but it should be noted that this diacritic *o* did not come into use until many centuries later than the period here under discussion.

The oppression which the Jews suffered in Egypt from Pharaoh signifies the slavery in which the Devil holds all mankind in heathendom; and the release whereby God removed them from that oppression signifies the freedom that God grants to His people when they are baptised. The Red Sea through which they passed signifies the baptismal font, which is sanctified by the blood shed in the slaying of Christ. Pharaoh and his army, which drowned in the Red Sea, signify the Devil and the sins which die away from every person in the water of baptism.

The most frequent symbols for *æ* were *ę, æ* and *e*; those for *œ* were *eo* (which went out of fashion about 1200), *ǿ, o* and later *ǫ́* and *ǿ*. When *æ* and *œ* fell together in pronunciation, symbols for the latter were sometimes used to express the result, in the early stages *ø* and *ǿ*, later more often *ǫ́* and *ǿ*, but the variant symbols for *æ*, among which *ę́* made a temporary appearance, gradually came to be the usual representation of the sound, and by 1400 *æ* itself was the predominant form.[109]

Some of the earliest scribes used *u* and *v* in more or less the same way as in Modern Icelandic, which prescribes the use of *u* as a vowel, *v* as a consonant. Others followed the modern rule only when these sounds occurred initially. Most scribes used the two characters indiscriminately, whether vocalic or semivocalic, but some adopted one or the other throughout their writing. Where *f* was most commonly written in medial and intervocalic positions (as in Modern Icelandic), this too may be represented in some early scripts by *u* or *v*, e.g. *haua, hava* for usual *hafa* 'to have'. Many fourteenth-century scribes adopted the custom of writing *v* (sometimes *w*) at the beginning of a word and *u* in the body and at the end of a word, whether the sound denoted was *u, ú* or *v*.[110]

j as a variant of *i* appears only exceptionally in the oldest manuscripts, but its use increased, especially in the fourteenth century. The practice of using *i* for the vowel and *j* for the semivowel or consonant, as in Modern Icelandic, was never followed. *j* might stand for *i, í* and *j*, but it was far more often used initially than elsewhere.[111]

In the very oldest manuscripts the vowels *e* and *o* were predominant in endings where *i* and *u* are now written. *i* and *u* (or *v*) soon made their appearance, however, and in time became established as final vowels, *i* earlier than *u*. In the thirteenth century some scribes seem to prefer *i* and *o* in endings, but by about 1300 *u/v* was mostly written for older *o*, and

[109] Holtsmark 1936, 10–11, 18–23; Lindblad 1954, 114–52, 308–16; Stefán Karlsson 1960, 83–93; Hreinn Benediktsson 1965, 56–72.
[110] Stefán Karlsson 1960, 72–74; Hreinn Benediktsson 1965, 25–26, 49–50.
[111] Stefán Karlsson 1960, 58; Hreinn Benediktsson 1965, 46.

---

(3) From *Heimskringla* (*Óláfs saga helga*, ch. 153), *c.*1260. Lbs. fragm. 82 (Kringla), fol. 1va.

Eɴ e*r* þ*eir* léco at scaktafli K*nutr* k*onungr oc* V*lfr* J*arl* þa léc k*onungr* fi*n*gr b*r*iot miki*ɴ*. Þa skækþi J*arl* af h*onom* riddara. K*onungr* bar aptr tafl h*ans oc* sagði at h*ann* scyldi aɴ*at* leika. Jarl reiddiz *oc* scá*t* niðr tafl borðino. Stóð upp *oc* gecc ib*r*ot. K*onungr* mælti. Rɴ*r* þ*v* nv ulfr hi*nn* ragi. J*arl* s*n*eri aptr við dyʀi*n*. *oc* mælti. Le*n*gra mu*n*dir þu re*ɴ*a i á*ɴ*e hælgo ef þ*v* qu*ę*mir þ*u*i við. Kallaþ*ir* þ*v* eigi þa Vlf hi*ɴ* raga e*r* ec lagða ti*l* at hialpa þ*er* er sviar b*o*rþo yðr se*m* hu*n*da.

fourteenth-century scribes in general use *o* only sporadically. Although *i* is the dominant spelling in final syllables, most scribes in this later period used *e* as well.[112]

Few scribes made a regular distinction between long and short vowels but most made some attempt to do so. In the earliest writing a long vowel was indicated by an accent over the letter, though this accent-mark was also apparently sometimes used to indicate stress. It was also not uncommon to mark an *i* with an accent in order to distinguish it from the minims of the characters *u, n* and *m*. Again, there were some scribes who used accents on no discernible pattern, sometimes placing them, for example, over short unstressed vowels. The use of the accent declined in the fourteenth century except as an *i*-marker, and in that period the Norwegian habit of doubling a vowel letter to indicate length (and sometimes in other circumstances) was increasingly adopted (*ii* is rare; the preferred form is *ij*). Long vowels written double sometimes had an accent-mark added. In the course of the fourteenth century it also became increasingly common to use ligatured *a+a (æ), o+o (œ)* and *w* when a scribe was keen to distinguish the long vowels *á, ó* and *ú*. As *é* became diphthongised, its pronunciation was gradually more and more often indicated by the spelling *ie*. Accents, more often a pair than a single mark, were sometimes added over ligatured vowels, and in the second half of the fourteenth century double accent-marks came to be used to indicate length over the letters *a, e, o, u/v* and *æ*.[113]

As mentioned earlier, *þ* was used in the earliest manuscripts, not only initially as it is today but also medially and finally, where *ð* is now written. *þ* (and later *ð*) was also used in certain consonant-clusters where this fricative later changed to *d* or *t* (cf. pp. 19–20 above). The character *ð* was derived from English script but came to Iceland from Norway, where it

[112] Lindblad 1954, 157–82, 308–16; Stefán Karlsson 1960, 65–66, 78; Hreinn Benediktsson 1962a.

[113] Lindblad 1952; Stefán Karlsson, 1960, 38–41, 51–53, 66–67, 69–70, 79–80, 85; Hreinn Benediktsson 1965, 60–61.

While they were playing chess, King Knútr and Earl Úlfr, the king made a seriously wrong move, and the earl took a knight from him. The king put his chess-piece back and said that he was going to make a different move. The earl became angry and dashed the chessboard to the floor. He stood up and walked off. The king said: 'Are you running away, Úlfr the Cowardly?' The earl turned round at the doorway and said: 'You would have run further in the Holy River (Helgeå) if you had been able to. You did not call me Úlfr the Cowardly when I did all I could to help you when the Swedes were beating you and your followers like dogs.'

was an early borrowing. In Icelandic writing it is first found in the first half of the thirteenth century, and it was gradually adopted by more and more scribes, using it instead of þ or alongside þ in medial and final positions. It was exceptional to use ð at the beginning of a word but its capital form Ð could be used as a decorative initial at the start of a chapter. Soon after 1300 medial and final þ was a rarity and by about 1400 it had disappeared altogether in these positions. It was replaced, however, not so much by ð as by d. The latter had itself begun to replace ð as the symbol for the medial and final fricative in the thirteenth century, and in the fourteenth it became the dominant spelling. This development also had a precedent in Norway where the fricative þ/ð was fast disappearing from speech.[114] In the fourteenth century, and even before 1300, ð was occasionally written for d, though it might very rarely occur in an initial position. After 1400 ð is seldom found in Icelandic script. The practice of writing ð was thus a short-lived phenomenon in early Icelandic.[115]

The recommendation of the First Grammatical Treatise that the short consonant k should be represented only by c was not followed. The earliest evidence suggests that a fair number of scribes observed the custom of writing k before front vowels and c elsewhere. The reason for this was probably not that k was regarded as a special symbol for palatal k, but rather the fact that before front vowels c no longer represented a k sound in contemporary Latin pronunciation. This differentiation between use of k and use of c was gradually dropped in the thirteenth century, though some scribes tended to prefer k in initial positions and c medially and finally, and in the fourteenth century c was only in restricted use.

In the oldest manuscripts and on into the thirteenth century q was usually written for k before v (written u or v or indicated by an abbreviation sign which stood for v and a following vowel). This practice, which accorded with a rule of Latin orthography, was gradually abandoned by Icelandic scribes.

[114] Seip 1955, 273–74, 289–91, 294.
[115] Lindblad 1954, 185–93, 308–16; Stefán Karlsson 1960, 116–17, Hreinn Benediktsson 1965, 21–22, 41, 43–44, 73–74.

---

(4) From *Njáls saga* (ch. 77), shortly after 1300. AM 468 4to (Reykjabók), fol. 39r.

Gvnnaʀ þrifr atgeiʀinn baðvm hondvm ok snyz at honvm skiott ok rekr ígegnvm hann ok kastar honvm a vollinn. þa liop vpp asbrandr broðir hans. Gvnnaʀ leGr til hans atgeiʀinvm. ok kom hann skildi fyrir sik. atgeiʀinn rendi ígegnvm skiolldín. en brotnvðv baðir handleGirnir. ok fell hann vt af veGinvm. aðr hafði Gvnnaʀ sert viij. menn en vegit þa .ij. þa fekk Gvnnaʀ sár .ij. ok saʻgʻðʻv þat allir menn at hann brygði ser hvarki við sár ne við bana. hann mellti til hallGerðar. fa mer leppa tva ór hári þinv.

In the fourteenth century it became common to write palatal *k* as *ki* before *æ* and before the *ö* which had previously been *ø*, though this spelling never appears before *i* and rarely before *e*. In these same positions *g* came correspondingly to be written *gi* (*kiðr*, *giæfa*, representing OldIcel. *kør* 'choice' and *gæfa* 'good luck' respectively).[116]

As noted earlier (p. 18), there were two kinds of *l*. In time it became more or less the rule that the dental *l* was written *ll* before *d* and *t*. For example, *valldi* was written for the dative of the noun *vald* 'power' but *valði* for the preterite of the verb *velja* 'to choose'; and this spelling remained even though the *ð* of *valði* later became *d* to give modern *valdi* 'I, (s)he chose'.[117]

Mention was made of the use of *x* and *z* at the end of the previous subsection (§ 2.1).[118] As well as using *z* in middle voice endings (cf. p. 31 above), fourteenth-century scribes commonly came to write it also in the superlative endings *-ast(-)* and *-ust(-)*. When these forms had no inflexional ending they were sometimes written *-az*, *-uz*; otherwise as *-azt(-)*, *-uzt(-)* or *-azst(-)*, *-uzst(-)*. The superlative ending *st* had been written *zt* when attached to a stem ending in a dental (*bezt* 'best', *min(n)zt* 'least'), but this spelling was only exceptionally extended to stems without a dental ending (e.g. *fremzt* 'foremost').[119]

The First Grammarian's recommendation of small capitals for long consonants was followed to some extent by most thirteenth-century scribes, and traces of the practice are visible down to about 1400. Some small capitals in this function were always rare; those that were in most frequent

---

[116] Lindblad 1954, 194–99, 308–16; Stefán Karlsson 1960, 127, 137–38; Hreinn Benediktsson 1965, 30–34, 77–79.

[117] Jakob Benediktsson 1960b.

[118] Lindblad 1954, 209–13; Stefán Karlsson 1960, 114, 118–19, 132, 142, 148–49, 154–55; Hreinn Benediktsson 1965, 74–76, 80.

[119] Jón Helgason 1926b, 73–75; Stefán Karlsson 1967, 18, 25, 55, and 1982, 73–75.

Gunnarr grabs hold of the thrusting-spear with both hands, turns briskly towards him, runs him through and throws him down to the ground [from the roof]. Then Ásbrandr, his [i.e., Þorbrandr Þorleiksson's] brother, leapt up. Gunnarr thrusts at him with the spear, but he covered himself with his shield. The spear went through the shield, and both Ásbrandr's arms (OR: both his upper and lower arm-bones) broke; he fell off the side of the building. By then Gunnarr had wounded eight men and killed those two. Then Gunnarr received two wounds; and everybody said that he flinched neither at wounds nor at death. He spoke to Hallgerðr: 'Give me two locks of your hair . . .'

and longest use were G, N and R. Writing double consonants to indicate length was also common from the earliest times, and in the early thirteenth century someone hit on the economic custom of marking a consonant as long by inserting a dot above its single-letter, lower-case form. This was particularly convenient over letters that had no ascenders, and along with the double writing of consonants it gradually became more or less standard practice. Long *k* was, however, an exception: it could be expressed by *c* or *k*, doubled or dotted, but from the earliest times it was also represented by *ck*, a spelling which became dominant in the course of the fourteenth century.[120]

Changes in pronunciation of individual phonemes were not generally reflected in spelling changes, though exceptions must be made in the case of sounds which fell together with sounds already in the language; see e.g. the examples given earlier in this subsection in connection with *æ* and *ö*. On the other hand, the force of scribal tradition meant that such mergers were often no more than sporadically represented in spelling. *rl* and *ll* fell together, as did *rn* and *nn*, after a long vowel, but the members of these pairs were generally kept distinct in script. In the fourteenth century, however, the common spellings *rll* and *rnn* are probably a joint indication of scribal custom and of the current pronunciation of *rl* and *rn*. The falling together is certainly evident in e.g. *kall* for *karl* '(old) man' and *eirn* for *einn* 'one', 'a certain'. In these combinations a *d* sound developed but it is rarely evident in script and then only in a 'back spelling' like *Orný* for the feminine personal name *Oddný*.[121] An exception to the general rule that isolative changes did not cause spelling changes is the case of *é* diphthongised to *ie* and often so spelt, as also shown earlier in this subsection.

Most combinative sound changes, on the other hand, did result in spelling changes. This did not always happen in regular fashion: established writing

[120] Lindblad 1954, 308–16; Stefán Karlsson 1960, 140–41; Hreinn Benediktsson 1965, 80–85.

[121] Jón Helgason 1927, 91–92; Stefán Karlsson 1982, 69, 71.

(5) From *Jónsbók*, 1363. AM 350 fol. (Skarðsbók), fol. 12ra.

Ef m*a*d*r* heim*ir* edr hysir utlægan man*n* etr m*e*d h*o*n*u*m e*d*r dreckr. bondi edr eín*n* hue*rr* an*n*aʀa ma*n*na. þa er sa sekr mörk uíd k*o*nu*n*g fy*rir* eína natt. en tueímr fy*rir* íj. nætr. En*n* ef h*a*nn er íjí. nætr medr h*o*n*u*m. ok er h*a*nn görr iɴan þ*er*s h*er*ads utlægr. þa er h*a*nn sekr þrettan morkum uíd k*o*nu*n*g. nema h*o*n*u*m se v vísa u*a*rgr er hysir. Alld*ri* sk*a*l þ*er*s sök meirí er hysír. en híns sok u*ar* þa er h*a*nn uar utlægr görr. En*n* syslu m*a*d*r* er skylldr at lysa utlegd h*a*ns samdægr*is* ᴁ þíngi e*r* h*a*nn ueít at h*a*nn hefir ut legd*ar* u*er*k un*n*ít.

habits and sometimes the influence of related word-forms that were unaffected by change could lead to the retention of an older orthography. Combinative changes that began to emerge by about 1400 or earlier have been touched on in the subsections on vowels and consonants, §§ 1.2.3 and 1.2.5 above. Some of these are evidenced in spelling, e.g. *vo* (*vó, uo, uó*) for older *vá*, *eing* for older *eng* (see p. 14 above). Evidence of pronunciation change can also be conveyed by misspellings. The old separate endings *-r* and *-ur* fell together with the introduction of epenthetic *u*, for example, and resulted both in the correct spelling *fagur* for older *fagr*, nom. sg. m. of the adj. meaning 'beautiful', and in the incorrect *flugr* for *flugur*, nom. and acc. pl. of the noun *fluga* 'fly'. A parallel development took place when *t* became *ð* at the end of a final unstressed syllable (see p. 19 above). The old endings *-at, -it, -ut* were then pronounced in the same way as the endings *-að, -ið, -uð*. In consequence the written forms appeared either as *ð* (or *d*), in accordance with the pronunciation, or as *t*, in accordance with scribal habit or as a misplaced archaism, seen e.g. in *hundrat* 'hundred'.[122]

A topic that requires some special mention is the influence of Norwegian orthography on that of Icelandic scribes in the thirteenth century and more particularly in the fourteenth. It was noted earlier in this subsection that Icelanders followed Norwegian example in adopting the letter *ð* and later abandoning it. Expression of *g* by *gh*, common in fourteenth-century Icelandic writing, was also of Norwegian origin. Originally *gh* stood for fricative *gh* (as in *sagha*, i.e., *saga* '(hi)story'), but most Icelandic scribes, if they used *gh* at all, tended to employ it for the stop as well (as in *þingh*, i.e., *þing* 'assembly'), though very rarely at the beginning of a word. Another probable loan from Norway was the use of *fu* medially for *f* before a vowel (*hafua, erfua*, i.e., *hafa* 'to have' and *erfa* 'to inherit'), a spelling that became common in the fourteenth century. Many Icelandic scribes also followed Norwegian practice in writing *æ* for *e*, especially in the

---

[122] Jón Helgason 1926b, 70–71; Stefán Karlsson 1982, 59, 64–65, 72.

If a man—whether he be a householder or any other man—harbours or houses an outlaw, or eats or drinks with him, he is answerable to the king for a fine of one mark for one night [of such harbouring], and of two marks for two nights. And if the outlaw spends three nights with him, and he has been made an outlaw in the district where the harbourer lives, then the latter is answerable to the king for a fine of thirteen marks, unless a sudden misfortune befalls him who does the harbouring. The harbourer's liability to a fine shall never be greater than was that of the outlaw when he was outlawed. Furthermore, the king's steward is obliged to give notice of the harbourer's fine at an assembly on the same day as he learns that he has committed this offence.

diphthongs (*æi, æy*); and after the sounds represented by *æ* and *œ* had fallen together in Icelandic, some Icelandic scribes tried to distinguish them in spelling as the Norwegians did. *u*-mutation was less a feature of Norwegian than of Icelandic, and Icelandic scribes sometimes wrote unmutated forms (e.g. *mannum* for *mǫnnum*, dat. pl. of *maðr* 'man'), most often in three-syllable words (e.g. *kallaðum* for *kǫlluðum*, first pers. pl. pret. indic. of *kalla* 'to call'). In Norwegian the initial *h*- in *hl, hr* was lost, and Icelandic scribes not infrequently wrote *l* and *r* in words they pronounced with *hl, hr* (e.g. *laupa, ross,* for *hlaupa* 'to run' and *hross* 'horse' respectively). An analogical *v* was introduced at the beginning of some forms in Norwegian, e.g. *vóx* for *óx*, first and third pers. sg. pret. indic. of *vaxa* 'to grow', *vurðu* for *urðu*, third pers. pl. pret. indic. of *verða* 'to become', and the same spelling is often found in Icelandic manuscripts. These and other features of Norwegian spelling are especially evident in the work of scribes who can probably be regarded as professionals. It was important for them to command an orthography that was acceptable throughout the realms of the king of Norway. For a time there appears to have been a lively demand in Norway for reading matter from Iceland, but after about 1350 it showed a marked decline.[123] (Cf. extracts 3–6.)

2.3 From the Black Death to the Reformation

About 1400 something of a hiatus begins in the history of Icelandic spelling. This is doubtless due in part to the plague years of 1402–1404 when scribes, whatever their status, suffered like the rest of the population. We can see, however, that the Norwegian features just enumerated disappeared almost entirely, though *fu* (which declined in use) and forms like *vurðu* (for *urðu* '(they) became') remained. Continuing Norwegian influence on Icelandic orthography was in any case not to be expected because the written language in Norway was by now far removed from that of Iceland. At the same time certain letter-forms and spelling habits

---

[123] Stefán Karlsson 1978 and 1979.

(6) From *Bevers saga*, c.1400. Holm. Perg. 4to nr. 6, fol. 4r.

Nv e*r* ath tala vm Gvíon J*ar*ll ath fyrsta dag maíj manadar arla sem þau lagu j sin*n*í sæng. þa taladi frvínn v*i*d Jarllin *ok* sagdizst v*er*a miok síuk. J*ar*ll fretti hue*r*n kra*n*kleika h*o*n hefdí *ok* bad ha*n*a segía ef ha*n*a lýstí nokku*rr*ar fædu. h*o*n sa*g*di. Ef ek fengí nytt villigalt*ar* hold þa væ*n*ti*r* mik ath ek fengi skíott heilsu mína. þ*at* veit gud s*e*gi*r* J*ar*ll ath ek sk*al* freista gíarna ef nokku*r*n kan*n* ek villí gault ath fáá. J*ar*ll stigu*r* nu vpp áá sín hest m*e*d eítt litíth sv*er*d *ok* skiold. huorkí hafdí h*an*n bryn*n*íu ne hialm.

that were already in decline before 1400 were now almost entirely abandoned. Some innovations in spelling that resulted from fourteenth-century sound changes had, however, become common currency and these became established in the course of the century that followed. But in general it may be said that the changes in spelling that took place between the Black Death and the Reformation were few and slight.

The old symbols ø and ǫ for ö were discarded, but ö continued to be expressed by a variety of letters, ð, o and au (or aʼ). æ-symbols that might be used for æ all disappeared, and æ was in general use throughout, though a few scribes preferred ę.[124]

There are no very obvious rules for distinguishing long and short vowels in this period, though there was a noticeable tendency to indicate long a in some way and ie became the predominant spelling for é. The single accent as a length mark almost completely disappeared, but it was customarily written as a marker over i and j, whatever their context, and this habit remained until foreign influence introduced a dot to replace the accent, a gradual process which culminated in the sixteenth century.[125] Where long vowels are distinguished in the script of this period it is by double letters (almost always ligatured except in íj for í and maybe further marked by a pair of accents), by a single letter marked by a pair of accents, and sometimes by a single letter with a superscript dot or a subscript hook.[126]

Most writers use only u in endings; o is rare. On the other hand, both e and i are common in endings, though many scribes show a preference for one or the other of them.[127]

---

[124] Stefán Karlsson 1960, 83–98; Ólafur Halldórsson 1968, xviii–xxxii, xliv.
[125] Lindblad 1952, 175.
[126] Stefán Karlsson 1960, 38–41, 51–53, 66–71, 79–80; Jónas Kristjánsson 1964, xix–xxiii, xli–xliv; Ólafur Halldórsson 1968, xx, xliv; Holm-Olsen 1910–86, xli–xliii, lx–lxiii.
[127] Hast 1960, 63–66; Stefán Karlsson 1960, 65–66, 78; Jónas Kristjánsson 1964, xxiii–xxiv, xlv; Holm-Olsen 1910–86, xlvii–xlix, lxiv–lxv.

It is now to be said of Earl Guion that, early on the first day of the month of May, as they lay in their bed, the lady spoke to the earl and said she was very sick. The earl asked what illness she was suffering from and begged her to say if there was any food for which she had an appetite. She said: 'If I had the fresh meat of a wild boar, then I expect that I would quickly recover my health.' 'God knows', says the earl, 'that I shall gladly see if there is any wild boar I can catch.' The earl now mounts his horse, taking one small sword and a shield; he had neither a mail-coat nor a helmet.

Small capitals indicating long consonants are a thing of the past, though N very occasionally appears for *nn* in the work of just a few fifteenth-century scribes.[128]

The combinative sound changes that began in the fourteenth century or earlier had increasing influence on fifteenth-century spelling. In addition, as time goes on, we find more and more evidence of the vowel changes that took place before *-gi* (see p. 14 above). Thus *ei* appears for *e*, as in *seigir* 'says' (sometimes spelt *seier*), and there is confusion between such words as *agi* 'awe', 'terror', and *ægi*, acc. sg. of *ægir* 'terrifier'; *daginn*, acc. sg. of *dag(u)rinn* 'the day', can be written *dæginn*.[129]

As noted in the previous subsection, the palatal pronunciation of initial *g* and *k* had often been indicated by writing *gi, ki* before *æ* and the product of old *ø*. This usage increased in the fifteenth century and was extended to these initial sounds before *e* as well (*giefa, kiemur*, i.e., *gæfa* 'good luck' and *kemur* (< *kømr*), third pers. sg. pres. indic. of *koma* 'to come').[130]

From about 1500 there are occasional spellings in which confusion of *i, í, ei* and *y, ý, ey* appear, even though the unrounding of *y* had not yet had any appreciable influence on the orthography in general.[131] (Cf. extracts 7–9.)

---

[128] Seelow 1981, 85, 95.
[129] Hast 1960, 60; Ólafur Halldórsson 1968, xviii, xxi; Seelow 1981, 98.
[130] Stefán Karlsson 1960, 127, 137–38.
[131] Hreinn Benediktsson 1977, 33–34; Guðvarður Már Gunnlaugsson 1994, 63–70, 91–98.

---

(7) From a wife's letter to her husband, *c*.1450. AM Dipl. Isl. Fasc. LXIV 17.

uillda eg at þi*er* letut illuga hafa kuíguna þa hína tuæuetru *og* af entut hana j fardaga siait nu til uín*nn*u ma*nn*ana at þeir fae klædín nog. uillda eg at jon*n* gudmu*n*dz son fengi .x. alna*r* uadmals. ef síra are gelldu*r* ocku*r* nocku*t* uadmal þa ska*l* ha*nn* fa nockrra skatta þar af en*n* profastu*r*ín*n* þat se*m* meíra e*r* j tiundi*r*na*r*. síaít nu t*il* allz se*m* þi*er* þeínckit at bezt gegní Hi*er* me*d* bífala eg ydr gudí j ualld *og* ha*ns* modu*r* maríe *og* sa*n*cte petre.

---

(8) From *Víglundar saga* (ch. 7), *c*.1500. AM 551 a 4to, fol. 2r.

þa at*ri* hv*n* olof *og* vn*n*ga d*o*ttv*r* e*r* helga h*et*. var hv*n* vetrí yn*n*gri en*n* k*et*ilridv*r*. lavgdvz þav oll sama*n* m*ed* gledi *og* skem*m*tan þessir*r* vngv me*nn*. en at hveriv gafn*n*i se*m* þav v*or*v hlotnadíz sva t*il* jafn*n*an. at þav v*or*v s*er* Uiglvndv*r og* K*et*ilridv*r* en*n* þav syskin s*er* t*r*avsti *og* helga. festi nv hv*or*t þeir*r*a Uiglvndar *og* K*et*ilridar *mick*la ast t*il* an*n*ars. tolvdv þ*at og* m*ar*gir at þ*at* þætri jafn*nr*ædi fy*r*ir flest*r*a hlvta saki*r*. þ*at* var jafn*an* e*r* þ*a*v v*or*v bædí sam*an* at hv*or*kí gadi an*n*ars en*n* horfa vp*p* æ an*n*at.

2.4 From the first printed books to the Enlightenment

The first books printed in Icelandic in the middle of the sixteenth century heralded a new period in the history of Icelandic spelling. Writers of manuscripts were undoubtedly influenced by the spelling of the printed word but their practice continued to be variable in a way that the language of printed books was not. At least during the long editorial career of Bishop Guðbrandur Þorláksson (1542–1627), the consistency of the printed language was firmly maintained.

The lettering of a language can pose problems for representation of it in print, as modern Icelanders have experienced with the advent of computers. The pioneers in the sixteenth century could not imagine embarking on a printed alphabet which did not include *þ*, and a special character had to be cut for it. Accents on the other hand were not used in the first centuries of Icelandic printing: the single accent had in fact disappeared as a length marker in manuscript, as mentioned earlier (p. 49), though a double accent or double dot was often used over the long vowels of Old Icelandic and their more recent equivalents. As noted above (p. 49), double letters were also a common way of indicating length in manuscript writing, and this custom was carried over into print, sometimes in ligatured forms, especially *æ* for *á* and *w* for *ú*, though for *í* the usual form in both script and print was *ij*. As before, spelling often gave no clue as to whether a vowel was long or short, but distinction between them gradually became commoner as the period advanced.[132]

---

[132] Jón Helgason 1929, 14; Lindblad 1952, 196–98; Bandle 1956, 25–34.

I would like you to let Illugi have the two-year old heifer and to hand it over during the moving days; see to it also that the labourers get enough clothes. I would like Jón Guðmundsson to receive ten ells of homespun cloth. If the Reverend Ari pays us for any of this cloth, then he is to receive some tax payments from the proceeds, and the rural dean is to receive the surplus in tithes. Look after everything as you think best. I commend you herewith to the care of God, His mother Mary, and Saint Peter.

Now Ólof herself had a young daughter whose name was Helga. She was a year younger than Ketilríðr. These young people all joined together for amusement and recreation, and in every game in which they took part it always turned out that Víglundr and Ketilríðr formed a separate pair, as did the brother and sister, Trausti and Helga. Víglundr and Ketilríðr now conceived a great love for one another, and many people said that this seemed a fitting match in most respects. It was always the case, when the two of them were together, that neither of them gave heed to anything apart from gazing at the other.

In this period, and to some extent before it, there was much irregularity in the use of single and double consonants, especially in clusters and at the end of unstressed syllables, where there was no distinction in pronunciation between long and short sounds. It was, for instance, very common to write and to print *ck* (= *kk*) both before and after other consonants (e.g. *Lycklar, Þanckar,* i.e., *lyklar* and *þankar,* nom. pl. of *lykill* 'key' and *þanki* 'thought' respectively); and endings in *-an* in some forms and with *-ann* in others came to be more and more often indiscriminately written single or double (e.g. *Konann,* i.e., *konan* 'the woman', and *Mannen,* i.e., *manninn,* acc. sg. of *maðurinn* 'the man').[133] A separate development was one which doubled letters of slender shape, *f* and tall *s* (ſ) (*haffa, Araſſon,* i.e., *hafa* 'to have' and the patronymic *Arason*), in cursive writing; doubling of this kind was common in Danish.

Capital letters had previously been rare save at the beginning of a paragraph or chapter but they now appear much more frequently. Some writers used them especially at the beginning of noun words, but examples of consistent use are hard to find. It is also often difficult to see the distinction between capital and lower-case letters in manuscript writing.[134]

---

[133] Bandle 1956, 91–112; Jón Helgason 1970.
[134] Jón Helgason 1929, 13; Bandle 1956, 19–22.

---

(9) From a deed of gift dating from 1545. AM Dipl. Isl. Fasc. L 21.

Þat gioru*m* vid olaf*ur* hialltaso*n* p*r*estu*r. og* arn*n*kell Gudvardzso*n* godu*m* m*o*nnu*m* kun*n*igt m*ed* þessu ockru opnu brefe at arum epter gudz burd M.d.xl. *og* v. J ytra gardzs horne i suarbadardal a midviku dagin i gagn*n* dôgu*m*. voru*m* vid i hia saau*m* og heyrdu*m* A. ord *og* handa band Jons. oddzso*n*ar. af ein*n*e alfu. en*n* þorgils p*r*estz sonar ha*n*s af an*n*are. at so f*yr*er skildu at h*ann* gaf h*on*u*m* x*c*. vpp i iordina ytra huarf i suarbadar dal til fullrar eignar þa strax . . . Og til san*n*inda hi*e*r v*m* sette f*yr* grei*n*du*r* jon oddzso*n* sitt insigli m*ed* ockru*m* in*n*siglu*m* f*yr*er þetta bref giôrt i sama stad deige *og* are se*m* f*yr*r seiger.

---

(10) From Bishop Guðbrandur Þorláksson's hymnal, *Ein ny Psalma Bok,* 1589. pp. aa iiij–v.

Med sama hætte hafa þ*ei*r enu Gômlu Forfedur vorer elskad og idkad/ þa Mælsnilld og þ*ad* *Skalldskapar Lag/ s*em* Noræ*n*u Mæle hæfer/ allra mest i Kuædum og Vijsum/ so s*em* openbert er/ ad þetta Noræ*n*u Mæl hefur Forprijs fram yfer môrg ôn*n*ur Tungumal/ þ*ad* vier af vitum/ i Skalldskapar Mælsnilld/ og Kuæda hætte/ huad san*n*liga er ein Gudz Gæfa/ þessu Noræ*n*u Mæle veitt og gefen/ huðria en*n* þo marger misbrwke/ þa er þ*ad* þ*ei*rra Synd og Skulld s*em* þ*ad* giôra. Og er hun þar fyrer ecke lastande/ helldur ættu Men*n* ad neyta hen*n*ar/ so Gude meige til Þocknunar og lofgiôrdar vera.

In the early part of this period *u* and *v* continued to be used interchangeably for the sounds represented by these letters, and the earlier custom of writing *v* initially and *u* in other positions was also common. A gradual development, however, saw the restriction of these characters to their particular function, with *u* written for the vowel and *v* for the consonant, at first in initial positions, subsequently in other positions as well. Much the same thing happened with *i* and *j*. In the earlier part of the period *j* was used initially, irrespective of the sound it stood for (*i, í* or *j*), but as time went on *i* came to be generally preferred for *i* and *í* in that position. As a capital letter, however, *J* could be used initially for any of the sounds involved, while in medial and final positions the letter *i* was most often exclusively used for the sounds represented by *i* and *j*.[135]

The 1540 print of Oddur Gottskálksson's New Testament translation had no symbol for *ö*; the sound was represented instead by *o* and sometimes *au*. In the second half of the sixteenth century some writers began to use *ø* on the Danish model, and this soon became the standard form in print, though some fonts had *ð*. In manuscripts *ð* and *au* were often used, as they had been earlier, but other letter-forms were also adopted: *ø*, borrowed from print, and more commonly *ð* and *ó*, each written sometimes with a tail descending from it. In the seventeenth century a few scribes imitated old manuscript usage and wrote *ǫ* for *ö*.[136]

---

[135] Jón Helgason 1929, 19, 23–24, 35, 46; Bandle 1956, 53–54, 64–65, 139, 179.
[136] Jón Helgason 1929, 27–28; Bandle 1956, 77–78.

We two, Ólafur Hjaltason, priest, and Arnkell Guðvarðsson, make known to people of good will with this open letter of ours that, one thousand five hundred and forty-five years after the birth of Christ, in Ytra-Garðshorn in Svarfaðardalur, on the Wednesday before Ascension Day, the two of us being present saw and gave ear to the words and handshake of Jón Oddsson on the one hand and his son Þorgils, priest, on the other, the effect thereof being that he gave into his full ownership from that moment ten hundreds of the Ytra-Hvarf estate in Svarfaðardalur... And in proof hereof the aforementioned Jón Oddsson placed his seal, with the seals of us both, on this deed, made in the same place, day and year aforesaid.

In the same manner did those ancient forefathers of ours love and cultivate the eloquence and poetic mode that befits the Norse language, most especially in poems and verses, clear as it is that this Norse language takes precedence over many other languages—as far as we can tell—in poetic eloquence and poetic form, which indeed is a particular gift of God granted and given to this Norse language; and though many may misuse this gift, that is the sin or fault of those who do so. The gift itself is in no way to be blamed for this; people should, rather, draw on it, so that it may redound to the pleasing and the praising of God.

o might appear in endings but most printed books used only *u*. On the other hand, *e* was often more frequent than *i* in this position. It has been suggested that this preference for *e* was due to the influence of Danish spelling but whether that was the reason is uncertain.[137] It is more likely that the phonetic value of the vowel thus represented in a relatively unstressed position was between those of *i* and *e* in a stressed position.

Some sound changes that were under way before this period began are now reflected in spelling with a fair degree of regularity. Thus, for instance, *ie* is commonly written for older *é* and *vo/uo* for older *vá*, and vowel changes before *ng, nk* are revealed by spellings such as *eing, ijng, äng* for older *eng, ing, ang*; these last spellings are commonly seen even in work by writers from the Vestfirðir (cf. pp. 12, 14 above).[138] The change of *ve* to *vö* is shown with some regularity (*Kuølld, huør, Jnguølldur*, i.e., *kvöld* 'evening', *hver* 'who', 'which', 'what', 'each', and the feminine personal

[137] Jón Helgason 1929, 20–23; Hægstad 1942, 48–49; Bandle 1956, 57–60, 68–69.
[138] Bandle 1956, 28, 31, 33, 41, 45–49, 78–79; Jón Helgason 1955a, 22–24.

(11) From Stefán Ólafsson's poem 'Um brullaupsreið Hornfirðinga' ('How they rode from Hornafjörður to the wedding in Álftafjörður') as preserved in a holograph manuscript dating from *c*.1650. Rostg. 121 4to LIIv.

    J Alftafirde war Brullauped Best
    Borin woru þangad Ølfaungen mest,
    þad Spyrst wm*m* Borg og By
    Bwrar fagna þvij,
    heyrdest þad lijka hornafiórd i,
    enn opt verdur hliótt epter gamaned.

    Þa Hornfirdijngarner heyrdu þad,
    huór sijna merina keyrde heim i hlad,
    mistu mein og swt,
    melium kostudu wt,
    hneptu i Buxur *og* wm*m* hǻlsen*n* klǻt.
    En*n* opt v*erdur* hli*ótt* e*pter* g*amaned.*

(12) From the second part (dating from 1720) of the original edition of Jón Þorkelsson Vídalín's book of sermons, *HVSSPOSTilla*, p. 202.

En*n* þad eg hefe ad framan*n* talad um*m* Heyrnar Skorten*n*/ þad sama vil eg um*m* Mælhelltena tala/ ad søn*n*u er hun stoor Vanse Lijkamans/ margur Ohlutvandur forsmæer þan*n*/ sem er svo Mæle faren*n*/ þeir hœda ad hønum/ herma epter þeim/ og læta miklu verr optast/ en*n* hiner sem þeir epter herma : þetta heiter ad lasta Skaparan*n*/ þvi han*n* hefur Man*n*enum Mæled gefed/ og sæ ed fremur þvilijkt Gudleyse/ hann er nærsta illa talande i ha*n*s Eyru*m*/ s*em* allt heyrer/ han*n* giører Mælsnylle sijna Þusundsin*n*um argare en*n* Brest hins Mælhallta.

name *Yngvöldur* (< *Yngveldr*, variant of *Yngvildr*)), and after 1600 spellings such as *fjegur, mieg* (i.e. *fjögur*, n. of *fjórir* 'four' and *mjög* 'very' (adv.)), which reflect the change of *jö* to *je*, are relatively frequent. There is sufficient evidence to show that at the beginning of the period *-r* could still be used for both the old endings *-r* and *-ur*, and that *-t* could be used for both earlier *-t* and *-ð* at the end of unstressed final syllables.[139]

In the oldest printed books the distinction between *i* and *y* was more or less correctly maintained, at least throughout the lifetime of Bishop Guðbrandur Þorláksson.[140] In most other writings from the period, evidence for the unrounding of *y, ý, ey* to *i, í, ei* respectively is far more striking than before, with writers using both *i* for *y* and *y* for *i*. Even though the old rounded pronunciation of *y* no longer existed in speech, the letter *y* continued to be written, and this scribal practice meant that more often than not *y* was bound to appear 'correctly' in writing. On the other hand, Ketill Jörundsson (1603–1670), parson at Hvammur í Dölum, who wrote many manuscripts, rejected *y* altogether and consistently wrote *i, í, ej* in every context.[141] His grandson, Árni Magnússon (1663–1730), at first followed his example, but when he became acquainted with medieval manuscripts he adopted *y* and for the most part succeeded in using it in accordance with old forms. His colleagues and most scholars since his time have aimed to do the same.

---

[139] Björn K. Þórólfsson 1925, xiii, xix, xxiv; Bandle 1956, 42–43, 156–57, 168–72.
[140] Bandle 1956, 71–76; Jakob Benediktsson 1960a, 160.
[141] Jón Helgason 1958, 96.

In Álftafjörður the best of weddings took place; the greatest supplies of liquor were brought there. News of it spreads far and wide; people welcome it. It also came to be heard of in Hornafjörður; but silence often falls after merriment.

When the people of Hornafjörður heard about it, each of them whipped his mare in from pasture; they abandoned suffering and sorrow, threw out the saddlecloths, buttoned up their trousers and put scarves round their necks. But silence often falls after merriment.

And I wish to say about impeded speech the same as what I have said above about hardness of hearing: that it is in truth a great bodily affliction. Many a dishonourable person despises the one whose speech is thus affected; they mock him, imitate him, and very often behave much worse than those whom they imitate. This amounts to laying blame on the Creator, for He has given language to man; and the person who perpetrates such godlessness is very ill-spoken in the ears of Him who hears all; he makes his eloquence a thousand times worse than any failing on the part of him whose speech is impeded.

The phonetic function of *z* was finally lost during this period, although some sixteenth-century writers still used it as before, that is, after the dentals in *ts, ds, ðs, lls, nns* and in middle voice and superlative forms. Gradually, however, it became customary to write *s* in its place, while at the same time some writers began to use *z* merely as a graphic variant of *s*, which is especially apparent in genitive endings of words whose stem did not end in a dental. In the seventeenth century the old rules governing the use of *z* were completely forgotten, and most writers abandoned the character except when it occurred in foreign names.[142] It did happen, however, that *z* was used for *st*, and we find spellings like *faz* (*fast* 'firm(ly)') and *ozr* (*ostur* 'cheese').[143]

Another change that took place gradually in this period and became apparent in spelling is the loss of the distinction between the two kinds of *l* that previously existed before *d*: *lld* had been customarily written for older *ld* and *ld* for older *lð*; now *ld* normally did service for both.[144]

There continued to be great irregularity in spelling, not least in handwritten work. It can be seen, however, that a few individuals created a more consistent orthography for their own use, and they also made innovations. Oddur Oddsson, parson at Reynivellir (*c*.1565–1649),[145] and the Rev. Ketill Jörundsson, mentioned above, are examples. Neither of these men laid down rules for spelling, and those which Jón Ólafsson from Grunnavík drafted remained unfinished and without influence.[146] One common element in the spelling conventions of these three writers was a consistent distinction that was made between the long and short vowels of early Icelandic, now separated by quality rather than quantity (cf. pp. 12–13 above).

A great many copies of medieval manuscripts were made in the seventeenth century and later. Some copyists did their best to follow the

[142] Bandle 1956, 166–67, 173–79.
[143] Jón Helgason 1926a, 72.
[144] Jakob Benediktsson 1960b.
[145] Stefán Karlsson 1981.
[146] Jón Helgason 1926a, 71–87.

(13) From an autograph manuscript (dating from 1767) of Eggert Ólafsson's *Búnaðarbálkur* ('Farming poem'). Lbs. 1513 4to, p. 43.

> Fýrer mig ein*n* eg ecke býgge,
> afspríng helldur og sveitungin*n*;
> epter mig vil eg verken*n* ligge,
> vid dœmen*n* ørvaz sein*n*re men*n*;
> ieg brúa, gerde, gautu rýd,
> graun*n*un*um* til þess veite lið.

spelling of their exemplars and indeed adopted orthographical features of early writing, sometimes using similar archaic forms even when not reproducing an old text. This last tendency could have catastrophic results, sometimes giving rise to a veritable mishmash of new and old, of contemporary spelling habits and antique manuscript orthography, the latter often misunderstood. Some scribes, for example, used *þ* in medial and final positions and made it do duty not only for *ð* but also for *d*; or they adopted Norwegian spellings, e.g. initial *l* and *r* for *hl* and *hr*. Sources showing such curiosities include books printed in Skálholt around 1690 containing not only medieval texts but an Icelandic version of *Gronlandia*, which Arngrímur Jónsson wrote in Latin between 1597 and 1602.[147] (Cf. extracts 10–12.)

2.5 The emergence of modern spelling

Eggert Ólafsson, who numbered educational reform among his many interests, produced a set of rules for Icelandic spelling in 1762. In some elements he followed contemporary convention, recommending for example *ck* for *kk* and *qv* for *kv*, and also final *e* (= *i*), spellings which had again become common in his century but have not since stood the test of time. He had become familiar with old manuscripts in Copenhagen and was much inclined to favour their orthography. He wished to adopt single-accent forms for the long vowels of Old Icelandic, *á, í, ó, ú, ý*, while for old *é* he recommended either *é* or *e* in preference to *ie*. He also advocated using *y* and *i* in accordance with the rules of the old language, and at the same time prescribed two kinds of *æ*, i.e., *æ* and *œ*, though he did not himself succeed in distinguishing clearly between them. Where pronunciation varied he emphatically recommended the use of older spellings, *ang* rather than *áng*, for example (cf. § 2.4 above), *iø* rather than *ie* (as in *fiør, kiør*, now *fjör* 'life' and *kjör* 'choice'), and *rf, lf*, rather than *rb, lb* (as in *arfur* 'inheritance', *álfur* 'elf'). In unstressed final positions he wished a distinction to be made between *-n* and *-nn*, as had been done earlier and is done today. He gave *z* a place instead of *st* in middle voice forms but otherwise restricted its use to foreign names (cf. extract 13).[148]

---

[147] Jón Helgason 1942, 32–35.
[148] Vilhjálmur Þ. Gíslason 1926, 147–67; Jón Helgason 1928, 61–65; Jón Aðalsteinn Jónsson 1959, 76–77.

Not for myself alone do I build, but rather for my offspring and fellow-countryman. I wish that my deeds should survive me; people of later times will be inspired by the examples. I build bridges, make fences, clear a path; I grant help to my neighbours to that end.

Eggert Ólafsson's spelling guide was not published, but it was circulated in copies and had a marked influence on the spelling of books printed in Icelandic in the next decades, and those books in turn had their influence on spelling habits. Older conventions remained in force at the printing press at Hólar as long as it continued to exist, that is, down to about 1800. The first published work to introduce a single accent over the vowels that had been long in Old Icelandic was the 1768 edition of *Konungsskuggsjá* printed at Sorø in Denmark,[149] but the influence of Eggert Ólafsson's rules is most clearly evident in books printed on Hrappsey from 1773 onwards, particularly in the publications of the first ten years or so. There was no thorough adherence to his principles, however, for *áng* and *eing* (cf. § 2.4) often appear in these prints, as well as *ie* for *é* and *-st* in the middle voice. Observance of the *i/y* distinction in a historically correct way was wavering, and no inclination to adopt *æ* was ever shown. The use of capital letters had hitherto been common in printed books but now it dwindled, being chiefly restricted to the start of a sentence and proper names.[150]

The publications of the Learned Arts Society (Lærdómslistafélag; 1779–1796) and of the Society for National Education (Landsuppfræðingarfélag; 1794–1827) brought increased fixity to Icelandic spelling. In 1794 the latter Society established a printing press at Leirárgarðar; it was later located at Beitistaðir and from 1819 to 1844 located on the island of Viðey, close to Reykjavík. The influence of Eggert Ólafsson's spelling rules is largely evident in the works issued by this press, but there are also some notable departures. Wherever it was typographically possible, a single accent was regularly placed over the long vowels of the old language, and *é* was introduced both where it was the old norm and after initial *g* and *k*

[149] Lindblad 1952, 198–200.
[150] Jón Helgason 1928, 64–74.

(14) From Magnús Stephensen's retrospective address on behalf of Iceland (personified as a woman) to the eighteenth century. Magnús Stephensen 1806, 520–21.

Stæra má eg mig annars af því, ad eg ein hefi svo fengid mitt málfæri vardveitt fram yfir flestar þjódir, frá því eg bygdist, árid 874, til þessa dags, ad þad enn má vyrdast sárlítid umbreytt eda gallad í munni og penna skynugra manna, á hvørju útlenda jafnvel furdad hefir, þegar t.d. franskt og þýdskt túngumál, eptir því, sem einhvør en ellstu skjøl í bádum, vardveitt frá byrjun 9du Aldar, sýna svo ad hafa umbreyttst til útfarar þinnar, ad þeirra daga Frønsku og Þýdsku skilja nú ecki nema rétt vel lærdir menn í þeim túngum. Þó eg nú ecki neiti, ad í daglegt tal og skyndi-rit, lædist opt inn blendin ord eda talshættir hjá sumum, veitir þó mørgum allhægt, ad bjóda mál mitt hreint og vítalaust fram.

(e.g. *géck, Kétill,* i.e., *gekk,* first and third pers. pret. sg. of *ganga* 'to walk' and the personal name *Ketill,* marking in that way the palatalising of *g* and *k* before *e*). Before *ng, nk* the vowels *a* and *i* were most often similarly accented and *au* (for older *ö*) was normally printed, but not usually *ei* (for older *e*) in the same position. In endings it now became the rule to print *i* rather than *e,* and around 1800 *j* began to be printed to represent the palatal glide in medial positions in place of the *i* that had been used before (so *gjøf,* now *gjöf* 'gift', and *byrja* 'to begin') (cf. extract 14).

Rasmus Rask, a Danish philologist and a great friend of Iceland, brought Icelandic spelling closer still to its modern guise both in his writings and in the editions for which he was wholly or partly responsible, chiefly from 1818 onwards. He set out his spelling rules in a booklet published in 1830.[151] Rask's view was that Icelandic spelling could in essentials serve equally well for both the old and the modern language. He used single accents over the old long vowels *á, í, ó, ú, ý,* but adopted a grave accent form *è* for *é* (= *je*). After *g, k* he found *e* sufficient (thus *gefa* 'to give', *kenna* 'to teach'). Where old *vá* changed to *vo* he wrote *vâ* (i.e., with a circumflex) in reproducing early Icelandic texts but *vo* if the text was a modern one (thus *vân* and *von,* both meaning 'hope'). He thought it correct to distinguish *æ* and *œ* in editions of early works but not otherwise. The character *ö* had previously long been used, like *ó,* to represent the long vowel *ó* but much less often for the sound usually represented by *ö*. Rask now made *ö* the norm for this sound in roman script but used the customary *ø* in Gothic (i.e., black letter) script. Rask wanted to omit epenthetic *u* (as in *tekr* 'takes'), but retained it in some words where he considered the *-ur* ending to be of ancient origin (e.g. *göltur* 'boar-pig', *fótur* 'foot'). As his norm for both Old and Modern Icelandic he wrote vowels with single accents and *au* and sometimes *ei* before *ng, nk,* though he finally came to

---

[151] Rask 1830.

I may indeed take pride in the fact that I alone have been able to keep my speech preserved more than most nations—from when I was first settled, in the year 874, to this day—in such a way that it may still seem very little changed or spoilt in the mouths and pens of discerning people; a fact at which even foreigners have marvelled, since the German and French languages—to judge from what some of the oldest manuscripts in both, preserved from the beginning of the ninth century, show—have changed up to the time of your passing [i.e., the eighteenth century, here addressed as a person] to such an extent that only people who are well and truly versed in those languages now understand the French and the German of those days. Although I do not deny that dubious words or phrases often infiltrate the daily speech and hastily produced writings of some, there are nevertheless many who find it reasonably easy to set forth my language in pure and faultless form.

question the propriety of such spellings in editions of Old Icelandic texts.[152] He found *c* and *q* superfluous and consequently wrote *drekka* 'to drink', *kvíga* 'heifer' and so on. On the other hand, he wished to reintroduce *z* for *s* where a preceding *t, d, ð* had been dropped, as in *vizka, vonzka, gæzka, talizt* (now *viska* 'wisdom', *vonska* 'anger', *gæska* 'goodness', and *talist*, pp. of *teljast* 'to be counted'). The greatest change in the overall appearance of written Icelandic was due to Rask's adoption of *ð*. This character had been used in print long before, in Olavius's edition of *Njáls saga* (1772), but only occasionally thereafter until it now appeared in texts for whose orthography Rask was ultimately responsible (cf. extract 15).[153]

Rask's spelling rapidly gained more or less general currency, chiefly because it was adopted in most of the publications of the Icelandic Literary Society (Hið íslenska bókmenntafélag), founded in 1816 on Rask's initiative, and in other publications prepared by Jón Sigurðsson (1811–1879) or under his aegis; Jón was president of the Literary Society for many years in the middle of the century. It may be noted that in 1828 the Society formally voted in favour of *ð* in its publications.[154] Nevertheless, down to about 1850 many books were still produced without the use of *ð*, particularly those printed in black letter. Since black letter was almost universal in books printed in Iceland down to 1844, and did not disappear for some decades after that,[155] the general public can hardly have come to make wide use of *ð* until the last years of the nineteenth century.

The nineteenth-century orthography that was most at variance with Rask's system was the one used, with occasional modifications, in the periodical *Fjölnir* from 1836 to 1843. It was expounded in two essays by Konráð Gíslason.[156] He held the view that the sole rule for spelling should be

[152] Rask 1832, 9–10.
[153] Jóhannes L. L. Jóhannsson 1922, 3–6; Jón Aðalsteinn Jónsson 1959, 77–79.
[154] [Rask] 1828, 41–44.
[155] Klemens Jónsson 1930, 122.
[156] [Konráð Gíslason] 1836 and 1837.

---

(15) From Rasmus Rask's presidential address to the Icelandic Literary Society. Rask 1828, 44–45.

Þetta gamla túngumál er það eina, sem Íslands þjóð hefir eptir af sínum fyrri blóma, hennar makt og eigin stjórn er farin, hennar skógarrækt og akryrkja er eingin, hennar skipagángr og ríkdómr er ekki töluverðr; ekkèrt er eptir henni til ágætis nema sú en forna túnga, sem allar þjóðir á Norðrlöndum þurfa að stunda, til þess að útskíra vel sín eigin túngumál. Þykir því vel verdt að bera sig að vanda hana af ýtrasta megni, og láta hana ekki umbreytast í neinu, nè spillast eðr tapast af hirðu leysi, og að vaka yfir því er einmidt þessa félags tilgángr og áform.

pronunciation, but that 'it was hardly worth the risk . . . of initiating such massive innovation' ('varla eígandi undir . . . að stofna til so mikillar níbreitni') as he thought was justified. It would 'overtax the eye' ('ofbiði auganu'), for instance, 'to see *aírið* for *ærið*, *aúvalt* for *ávalt*, *oúheppið* for *óheppið*', and so on (*ærið* and *óheppið* are the nom. and acc. sg. n. forms of the adjectives *ærinn* 'sufficient', 'considerable' and *óheppinn* 'unlucky' respectively; *ávalt* (now *ávallt*) = 'always'). The chief departures from Rask's system in the practice of the *Fjölnir* men were as follows: the letter *y* was dismissed; *eí* was written for *ei/ey*; *je* was written instead of *è* or *é*; before *gi, gj* they wrote *eí* (as in *veígið, seígja*, now respectively *vegið*, second pers. pl. pres. of *vega* 'to weigh', and *segja*, inf., 'to say'); they had initial *gj, kj* where the pronunciation seemed to warrant them (as in *Gjísli, kjenna*, for the personal name *Gísli* and *kenna* 'to teach' respectively); they wrote -*ur* everywhere in endings. They had some additional pronunciation-based forms, such as *hvur* for *hver* 'who', 'each', etc., and *abl* for *afl* '(physical) strength'. They kept *z*, however, not only where Rask advocated its use but also in genitive forms like *Lopz* (for *Lofts*, gen. sg. of the personal name *Loftur*), *lanz* (for *lands*, gen. sg. of *land* 'land') and *orz* (for *orðs*, gen. sg. of *orð* 'word'). Konráð Gíslason's spelling system met criticism and no very enthusiastic response; the *Fjölnir* group abandoned it in 1844.[157]

Halldór Kr. Friðriksson (1819–1902) taught Icelandic at the Grammar School in Reykjavík for nearly half a century (1848–1895). He had been involved with *Fjölnir* in the last years of its existence and throughout his career he taught what was essentially the spelling adopted by the editors of that periodical in 1844. He gave a detailed account of its principles in a book published in 1859.[158] This spelling, often referred to as the 'school spelling', was based on Rask's recommendations but departed from them

---

[157] [Konráð Gíslason] 1844; Jóhannes L. L. Jóhannsson 1922, 7–8; Jón Aðalsteinn Jónsson 1959, 79–84.
[158] Halldór Kr. Friðriksson 1859.

This ancient language is the one thing that the Icelandic nation has left of its former flourishing state. Its power and self-government are gone; its forestry and agriculture are non-existent; its shipping and wealth are of no account. Nothing remains that might reflect its merit save that ancient language which all the nations of Scandinavia need to study in order to account adequately for their own languages. It therefore seems well worth making the greatest possible effort to treat it with care, and to prevent it from changing in any respect and from becoming spoilt or lost through negligence; and to watch over it is precisely the purpose and aim of this Society.

on various points. In requiring *je* rather than *è* or *é* and the epenthetic *u* in *-ur(-)*, the system came closer to contemporary pronunciation than Rask's and indeed to that of many of Rask's predecessors. On the other hand, it showed more respect for etymology and in some degree for archaism inasmuch as the old short vowels before *ng, nk* were not to be written in any way that showed their new quality in these positions. The 'school spelling' also distinguished not only between *i, í, ei* and *y, ý, ey* respectively, but also between two forms of *æ*, i.e., *æ* and *œ*; choice between these last two depended on etymology, *æ* in derivations from words with old *á*, *œ* in those from words with old *ó*. Rules for the use of *z* were rather similar to Rask's but applied more widely, though not so far as to prescribe *z* in genitive forms, which had been the original practice of the *Fjölnir* group. It should finally be mentioned that the 'school spelling' also relied on etymology to decide whether a consonant immediately before another consonant should be written single or double, though Old Icelandic orthography did not lend much support to this principle. Thus *þekkt* came to be the correct form for the nom. and acc. sg. n. of the adj. *þekkur* 'agreeable', but *spakt* in the same cases, number and gender of *spakur* 'wise'; *stokknir* was similarly the correct form for the nom. pl. m. of the pp. of *stökkva* 'to jump', but *roknir* for the same case of the pp. of *rjúka* 'to emit smoke or steam' (cf. extract 16).[159]

A few scholars moved farther towards the archaic than the 'school spelling' promoters, not least by dropping epenthetic *u*, but most people found themselves in difficulties if they attempted to follow their example. Most texts published in Icelandic in the second half of the nineteenth century essentially followed the 'school spelling', though the distinction of *æ* and *œ* never became a general feature, and the spelling of the written language among the population at large remained relatively diverse and

[159] Jóhannes L. L. Jóhannsson 1922, 7–11; Jón Aðalsteinn Jónsson 1959, 84–87.

(16) From Halldór Kr. Friðriksson's spelling guide. Halldór Kr. Friðriksson 1859, 35–36.

Það virðist því rjettasta reglan að rita samkvæmt upprunanum, eptir þeim myndum, sem orðin fá, er þau verða íslenzk eða norrœn, eða eru tekin inn í norrœnuna; en framburðurinn má þó eigi vera þvert á móti rithættinum; vjer megum eigi rita þá stafi, sem hvorki heyrast í framburðinum, nje verða látnir heyrast; og þessi virðist vera aðalundirstaðan fyrir rithætti fornmanna, þótt víða út af beri, og þessi virðist undirstaðan enn, eptir því sem flestir rita, þótt hún í mörgu sje aflöguð; . . . tungan hefur að nokkru breytzt á hinum síðustu fimm öldum, og því verður og að breyta til um rithátinn, með því að enginn getur hugsað til, að fœra allt aptur til hinna fornu myndanna, heldur verður að taka tunguna, eins og hún nú er orðin.

in some degree influenced both by current pronunciation and by older spelling habits. A few men attempted to introduce reforms which would bridge the gaps still to be seen between pronunciation and spelling. The most notable of these was Björn M. Ólsen (1850–1919), the first professor of Icelandic in the University of Iceland, founded in 1911. He sought to simplify the spelling, partly, as he thought, to make it easier to learn. The most important change he advocated was the abolition of *y* and *z*. Icelandic orthography was a subject of hot debate around 1890, especially between Björn M. Ólsen and Halldór Kr. Friðriksson, who stood by the 'school spelling' for which he had been chiefly responsible.[160]

Disputes about Icelandic spelling have often erupted since then, and opinions have differed over basic principles: should etymology be the decisive factor or should pronunciation and ease of acquisition take precedence? In 1898 spelling rules were introduced, the so-called 'journalists' spelling', by the newspaper editors, Jón Ólafsson (1850–1916) and Björn Jónsson (1846–1912). Thereafter many teachers asked for guidance from the authorities on what spelling should be taught in schools, but it was not until 1918 that a set of instructions was issued. More regulations were issued in 1919 and again in 1974, with minor amendments in 1977.

The changes back and forth in the spelling regulations of the twentieth century relate to the same questions as those which gave grounds for argument in the nineteenth century: Is *je* preferable to *é* or *é* to *je*? Should *z* be used and if so by what rules? When should a consonant before another consonant be written double? Disputes on these and other questions of still less significance have often been more heated than the occasion warranted.[161]

---

[160] Björn M. Ólsen 1889; Jóhannes L. L. Jóhannsson 1922, 11–12; Jón Aðalsteinn Jónsson 1959, 88–94.
[161] Jóhannes L. L. Jóhannsson 1922, 12–33; Jón Aðalsteinn Jónsson 1959, 94–119.

The most strictly correct approach thus seems to be to write with etymology in mind, following those forms which the words acquire when they become Icelandic or Norse, or are adopted into Norse. But pronunciation should not be directly contrary to spelling: we should not write those letters which are neither heard, nor allowed to be heard, in pronunciation; and this seems to be the main foundation on which the spelling of the ancients was based, even though it was frequently departed from; and this still seems to be the foundation, to judge from how most people write, although it is in many respects impaired; ... the language has changed to some extent in the past five centuries, and it is therefore necessary to make adjustments with regard to spelling, for no-one can envisage a wholesale removal back to the ancient forms; the language should, rather, be taken for what it has now become.

3. One language

The sections above on pronunciation and sound changes have shown the great changes that have taken place in Icelandic since the country was first settled. The most radical of these, however, were all for the most part completed by the early seventeenth century. Some other sound changes, not effective in every part of the country, have fluctuated in extent and distribution in past centuries. Research in this field has been chiefly limited to study of the distribution of pronunciation features as recorded in recent decades.[162] Still less has been published on the dialect distribution of inflexional forms and vocabulary, even though we know that in earlier centuries, no less than in the twentieth, local bounds were set to a good many words and word-forms.[163] Differences in language usage from one part of Iceland to another are, however, very slight, especially if seen in contrast to the dialectal differences that developed in neighbouring languages. This may seem surprising at first sight, given the scattered and widespread pattern of Icelandic settlement.

What is more distinctive of Icelandic than anything else is, on the one hand, this virtual absence of regional variation and, on the other, the minimal difference between Old and Modern Icelandic in the inflexional system and lexicon. There are many reasons for this, and none of them tells the whole story. The following are those that may reasonably be counted the most valid.

From the time when writing was first introduced, the practice of reading was entrenched among Icelanders. Among the books that were read, heard and re-told were the greatest works of medieval Icelandic literature, and in this way they undoubtedly played their part in the preservation of the lexicon and inflexions of the ancient language. Iceland's geographical situation and the comparatively few immigrants who arrived there after the time of the settlement meant that foreign influences were not nearly as strong in Iceland as in many other countries. Distances within Iceland were great, but there was an astonishing amount of travel and movement within the country, notably the annual ride to the Alþingi, a prominent feature of Icelandic life for centuries and one which, in the early period at

---

[162] Björn Guðfinnsson 1946 and 1964; Dahlstedt 1958a and b; Hreinn Benediktsson 1961–62b; Jón Aðalsteinn Jónsson 1964, 69–80; Kristján Árnason and Höskuldur Þráinsson 1983; Höskuldur Þráinsson and Kristján Árnason 1984; Guðvarður Már Gunnlaugsson 1987a; Höskuldur Þráinsson and Kristján Árnason 1986.

[163] Jón Aðalsteinn Jónsson 1953; Jón Helgason 1960; Jón Aðalsteinn Jónsson 1964, 65–69, 80–85.

least, brought together large numbers of people from all parts. Wealthy families in Iceland often owned estates in many different districts and they intermarried with families who lived far from their own chief homestead. There were few schools in Iceland; for centuries indeed there were only two, and for much of the nineteenth century only one, which meant that pupils foregathered from every corner of the country. Clergy often worked in parishes remote from their own place of origin and they often moved from one rural district to another far away. When fisheries were developed to serve the export market many people joined in seasonal fishing work in the south and west of the country, coming to the fishing stations from all parts and returning home for summer haymaking. Vagrants travelled all over the country; they naturally visited the bishops' sees, places to which many other people also had errands, including, in pre-Reformation times, pilgrims to the shrines of the saints lying at rest in the cathedrals. All this traffic, along with the contacts that inevitably existed between neighbouring districts, certainly contributed to linguistic levelling. Most of the major sound changes in fact spread over the whole country in just a few generations. On the other hand, there were some innovations that arose in one or another part of the country and gained some currency but in the long run were unable to compete with old features which survived intact elsewhere.[164]

In the matter of orthography we may recall that early in the history of writing Icelandic an anonymous author attempted to provide spelling rules which in fact were remarkably well adapted to the sound system of his contemporary twelfth-century speech. His rules were, however, nowhere followed precisely in any of our extant sources, and spelling in the following centuries was characterised by inconsistency and the absence of observable rules. This irregularity was partly due to conflict between novel changes in pronunciation and old scribal habits.

From the late eighteenth century onwards, efforts to standardise spelling had some effect, and although changes and comparatively radical deviations were advocated in a few exceptional cases, it is on the whole true to say that a generally accepted spelling system was established in the nineteenth century. The outcome is a spelling which is essentially etymological and takes account of only a few of the changes in pronunciation that have occurred since 1400 and, indeed, makes no concession to some changes that were already effective before that date. Among other things this means that the national spelling is a kind of common denominator for regional

---

[164] Helgi Guðmundsson 1977.

variations: in the few cases of different dialectal pronunciation the standard spelling reflects the old way of saying a word, even though that old way remains the habit of comparatively few speakers (as in *langur* 'long' (adj.) and *daginn*, acc. sg. of *dagurinn* 'the day'). The archaising tendency which proposed two symbols for the sounds underlying *æ* (i.e. *æ* and *œ*), which had merged in the thirteenth century, was abandoned. On the other hand, it has become established writing practice to distinguish, or to try to distinguish, between *i, í, ei* and *y, ý, ey* respectively, in accordance with the old pronunciation of these sounds; and similarly between *n* and *nn* in final unstressed position, despite the fact that both these distinctions in pronunciation disappeared through merger many centuries ago. Modern Icelandic spelling thus reveals the influence of pronunciation and scribal habit from different periods of the past, and in some cases it marks a return to early medieval times.

In the last two centuries there has also been something of a return to Old Icelandic forms in inflexions and vocabulary; instances have been noted in §§ 1.3 and 1.4 above. Conscious cultivation of the language has been largely responsible for this movement. If we disregard the many neologisms of Modern Icelandic, the present-day written language is in many respects closer to Old Icelandic than to the Icelandic found in most printed books published between 1540 and 1800. This development of the language would hardly have been as thoroughgoing as it has been without the progress made in education and school-attendance; but it also owes much to the interest generally taken by Icelanders in language and use of language, and to the fact that most of the population have felt it an honour to possess a language so little changed from its ancient form that they have minimal trouble in understanding the literature created by their forebears centuries ago.[165]

---

[165] In the second paragraph of § 2.2, above, it is stated that there is no trace of any distinction made in writing between nasal and oral vowels. This was the conclusion of Hreinn Benediktsson 1965, 60, and 1972, 130–31. On the other hand, de Leeuw van Weenen, 1993, 60–61, has claimed to find in the orthography of the Icelandic Homily Book, *c*.1200, indications that, in the exemplar (or exemplars) of that codex, a special symbol was used for nasal *ó*. Cf. *Stafkrókar* 75.

Bibliography

NOTE. The alphabetical order used here is Icelandic rather than English, following that of *An Icelandic–English Dictionary* by Richard Cleasby and Gudbrand Vigfusson, 2nd ed. (Oxford, 1957). Icelanders are listed by their first names. It should be noted that, in the alphabetical sequence, Icelandic patronymics take precedence over additional forenames; thus, Halldór Ármann Sigurðsson is listed after, rather than before, Halldór Halldórsson.

Alexander Jóhannesson 1923–1924. *Íslenzk tunga í fornöld.* Reykjavík.

Arngrímur Jónsson 1950–57. *Opera latine conscripta* I–IV. Ed. Jakob Benediktsson (Bibliotheca Arnamanæana IX–XII). Copenhagen.

Árni Böðvarsson 1964. 'Viðhorf Íslendinga til móðurmálsins fyrr og síðar'. In *Þættir um íslenzkt mál*, 177–200. Reykjavík.

Ásgeir Bl. Magnússon 1959. 'Um framburðinn rd, gd, fd'. *Íslenzk tunga. Tímarit um íslenzka og almenna málfræði* 1, 9–25. Reykjavík.

Ásgeir Bl. Magnússon 1981. 'Um sérhljóðabreytingar á undan samhljóðaklösum með *l-i*'. In *Afmæliskveðja til Halldórs Halldórssonar 13. júlí 1981*, 24–38. Reykjavík.

Ásgeir Bl. Magnússon 1989. *Íslensk orðsifjabók.* Reykjavík.

Baldur Jónsson 1976. *Mályrkja Guðmundar Finnbogasonar.* Reykjavík.

Bandle, Oskar, 1956. *Die Sprache der Guðbrandsbiblía. Orthographie und Laute. Formen* (Bibliotheca Arnamagnæana XVII). Copenhagen.

Bandle, Oskar, 1973. *Die Gliederung des Nordgermanischen.* Beiträge zur nordischen Philologie I. Basel.

Bjarni Vilhjálmsson 1944. 'Nýyrði í Stjörnufræði Ursins'. *Skírnir. Tímarit Hins íslenzka bókmenntafélags* CXVIII, 99–130. (Reprinted 1985 in *Orð eins og forðum. Greinasafn eftir Bjarna Vilhjálmsson, gefið út í tilefni af sjötugsafmæli hans 12. júní 1985*, 1–29.) Reykjavík.

Björn Guðfinnsson 1941. 'Málbótastarf Baldvins Einarssonar'. *Andvari* 66, 64–78. Reykjavík.

Björn Guðfinnsson 1946. *Mállýzkur* I. Reykjavík.

Björn Guðfinnsson 1947. *Breytingar á framburði og stafsetningu.* Reykjavík.

Björn Guðfinnsson 1964. *Um íslenzkan framburð. Mállýzkur* II. Ed. by Ólafur M. Ólafsson and Óskar Ó. Halldórsson (Studia Islandica 23). Reykjavík.

Björn M. Ólsen 1889. 'Um stafsetning'. *Tímarit um uppeldi og menntamál* 2, 3–24. Reykjavík.

Björn K. Þórólfsson 1925. *Um íslenskar orðmyndir á 14. og 15. öld og breytingar þeirra úr fornmálinu með viðauka um nýjungar í orðmyndum á 16. öld og síðar.* Reykjavík.

Björn K. Þórólfsson 1929a. 'Kvantitetsomvæltningen i islandsk'. *Arkiv för nordisk filologi* 45, 35–81. Lund.

Björn K. Þórólfsson 1929b. 'Nokkur orð um hinar íslensku hljóðbreytingar é > je og y, ý, ey > i, í, ei'. In *Studier tillägnade Axel Kock*, 232–43. Lund.

Chapman, Kenneth G., 1962. *Icelandic–Norwegian Linguistic Relationships. Norsk tidsskrift for sprogvidenskap*, suppl. bind. VII. Oslo.

Dahlstedt, Karl-Hampus, 1958a. 'Isländsk dialektgeografi. Några synpunkter'. *Scripta Islandica* 9, 5–33. Uppsala.

Dahlstedt, Karl-Hampus, 1958b. 'Íslenzk mállýzkulandafræði. Nokkrar athuganir'. *Skírnir. Tímarit Hins íslenzka bókmenntafélags* CXXXII, 29–63. Reykjavík.
Finnur Jónsson 1901. 'Íslenskan'. *Árný gerð út af Fjelagi íslenskra stúdenta í Kaupmannahöfn*, 49–69. Copenhagen.
Fischer, Frank, 1909. *Die Lehnwörter des Altwestnordischen*. Palaestra LXXXV. Berlin.
Guðvarður Már Gunnlaugsson 1987a. 'Íslenskar mállýskurannsóknir. Yfirlit'. *Íslenskt mál og almenn málfræði* 9, 163–74. Reykjavík.
Guðvarður Már Gunnlaugsson 1987b. 'Skrá um rit er varða íslenskar mállýskur'. *Íslenskt mál og almenn málfræði* 9, 175–86. Reykjavík.
Guðvarður Már Gunnlaugsson 1994. *Um afkringingu á /y, ý, ey/ í íslensku* (Málfræðirannsóknir 8). Reykjavík.
Gunnar Karlsson 1965. 'Um aldur og uppruna kv-framburðar'. *Íslenzk tunga. Tímarit um íslenzka og almenna málfræði* 6, 20–37. Reykjavík.
Halldór Kr. Friðriksson 1859. *Íslenzkar rjettritunarreglur*. Reykjavík.
Halldór Halldórsson 1950. *Íslenzk málfræði handa æðri skólum*. Reykjavík.
Halldór Halldórsson 1964a. 'Nýgervingar í fornmáli'. In *Þættir um íslenzkt mál*, 110–33. Reykjavík.
Halldór Halldórsson 1964b. 'Nýgervingar frá síðari öldum'. In *Þættir um íslenzkt mál*, 134–57. Reykjavík.
Halldór Halldórsson 1968. 'Synd—An Old-Saxon loanword'. *Scientia Islandica* 1, 60–64. Reykjavík.
Halldór Halldórsson 1969. 'Some Old Saxon loanwords in Old Icelandic poetry and their cultural background'. In *Festschrift für Konstantin Reichardt*, 109–26. Bern.
Halldór Halldórsson 1971. 'Nýyrði frá síðari öldum'. In Halldór Halldórsson, *Íslenzk málrækt. Erindi og ritgerðir*, 212–44. Reykjavík.
Halldór Ármann Sigurðsson 1982. 'Smásaga vestan af fjördum'. *Íslenskt mál og almenn málfræði* 4, 285–92. Reykjavík.
Hast, Sture, ed., 1960. *Harðar saga* (Editiones Arnamagnæanæ A6). Copenhagen.
Haugen, Einar, ed., 1950. *First Grammatical Treatise. The Earliest Germanic Phonology. An Edition, Translation and Commentary* (Language Monograph 25). Baltimore, Maryland (2nd ed. London, 1972).
Haugen, Einar, 1976. *The Scandinavian Languages. An Introduction to their History*. London.
Helgi Guðmundsson 1959. 'Máki, mákur'. *Íslenzk tunga. Tímarit um íslenzka og almenna málfræði* 1, 47–54. Reykjavík.
Helgi Guðmundsson 1960. 'Sklokr'. *Íslenzk tunga. Tímarit um íslenzka og almenna málfræði* 2, 51–56. Reykjavík.
Helgi Guðmundsson 1969. 'Fuglsheitið jaðrakan'. In *Afmælisrit Jóns Helgasonar 30. júní 1969*, 364–86. Reykjavík.
Helgi Guðmundsson 1970. 'Um slafak og marinkjarna'. *Fróðskaparrit. Annales Societatis scientiarum Færoensis* 18, 192–205. Tórshavn.
Helgi Guðmundsson 1972. *The Pronominal Dual in Icelandic*. University of Iceland. Publications in Linguistics 2. Reykjavík.

Helgi Guðmundsson 1977. 'Um ytri aðstæður íslenzkrar málþróunar'. In *Sjötíu ritgerðir helgaðar Jakobi Benediktssyni 20. júlí 1977*, 314–25. Reykjavík.
Helgi Guðmundsson 1997. *Um haf innan. Vestrænir menn og íslenzk menning á miðöldum*. Reykjavík.
Hermann Pálsson 1952. 'Keltnesk mannanöfn í íslenzkum örnefnum'. *Skírnir. Tímarit Hins íslenzka bókmenntafélags* CXXVI, 195–203. Reykjavík.
Hermann Pálsson 1996. *Keltar á Íslandi*. Reykjavík.
Hoffory, J., 1883. *Oldnordiske consonantstudier*. Copenhagen.
Holm-Olsen, Ludvig, ed., 1910–86. *Det Arnamagnæanske Håndskrift 81a Fol. (Skálholtsbók yngsta)*. Oslo.
Holtsmark, Anne, 1936. *En islandsk scholasticus fra det 12. århundre*. Skrifter utgitt av Det Norske Videnskaps-Akademi i Oslo II. Hist.-Filos. Klasse. 1936. No. 3. Oslo.
Hreinn Benediktsson 1959. 'The vowel system of Icelandic: A survey of its history'. *Word* 15, 282–312. New York. (Republished in Hreinn Benediktsson 2002, 50–73.)
Hreinn Benediktsson 1961–62a. 'Óákv. forn. nokkur, nokkuð'. *Íslenzk tunga. Tímarit um íslenzka og almenna málfræði* 3, 7–38. Reykjavík. (Republished in revised form and in English, in Hreinn Benediktsson 2002, 470–519.)
Hreinn Benediktsson 1961–62b. 'Icelandic dialectology: Methods and results'. *Íslenzk tunga. Tímarit um íslenzka og almenna málfræði* 3, 72–113. Reykjavík.
Hreinn Benediktsson 1962a. 'The unstressed and the non-syllabic vowels of Old Icelandic'. *Arkiv för nordisk filologi* 77, 7–31. Lund. (Republished in Hreinn Benediktsson 2002, 74–91.)
Hreinn Benediktsson 1962b. 'Islandsk språk'. In *Kulturhistorisk leksikon for nordisk middelalder* VII, 486–93. Reykjavík.
Hreinn Benediktsson 1964a. 'Old Norse short *e*: One phoneme or two?'. *Arkiv för nordisk filologi* 79, 63–104. Lund. (Republished in Hreinn Benediktsson 2002, 111–41.)
Hreinn Benediktsson 1964b. 'Upptök íslenzks máls'. In *Þættir um íslenzkt mál*, 9–28. Reykjavík.
Hreinn Benediktsson 1964c. 'Íslenzkt mál að fornu og nýju'. In *Þættir um íslenzkt mál*, 29–64. Reykjavík.
Hreinn Benediktsson 1965. *Early Icelandic Script as Illustrated in Vernacular Texts from the Twelfth and Thirteenth Centuries* (Íslenzk handrit. Icelandic Manuscripts. Series in Folio, vol. II). Reykjavík.
Hreinn Benediktsson 1967–68. 'Indirect changes of phonological structure: Nordic vowel quantity'. *Acta Linguistica Hafniensia* XI:1, 31–65. Copenhagen. (Republished in Hreinn Benediktsson 2002, 164–89.)
Hreinn Benediktsson 1969. 'On the inflection of the ia-stems in Icelandic'. In *Afmælisrit Jóns Helgasonar 30. júní 1969*, 391–402. Reykjavík.
Hreinn Benediktsson, ed., 1972. *The First Grammatical Treatise. Introduction. Text. Notes. Translation. Vocabulary. Facsimiles* (University of Iceland. Publications in Linguistics 1). Reykjavík.
Hreinn Benediktsson 1977. 'An extinct Icelandic dialect feature: *y* vs. *i*'. In *Dialectology and Sociolinguistics. Essays in honor of Karl-Hampus Dahlstedt*

19 April 1977 (Acta Universitatis Umensis. Umeå Studies in the Humanities 12), 28–46. Umeå. (Republished in Hreinn Benediktsson 2002, 214–26.)

Hreinn Benediktsson 1979. 'Relational sound change: *vá* > *vo* in Icelandic'. In *Linguistic Method. Essays in honor of Herbert Penzl*, 307–26. The Hague. (Republished in revised form in Hreinn Benediktsson 2002, 227–42.)

Hreinn Benediktsson 2002. *Linguistic Studies, Historical and Comparative*. Ed. Guðrún Þórhallsdóttir, Höskuldur Þráinsson, Jón G. Friðjónsson and Kjartan Ottósson. Reykjavík.

Hægstad, Marius, 1942. *Vestnorske maalføre fyre 1350. II. Sudvestlandsk. 2. Indre sudvestlandsk. Færøymaal. Islandsk. Tridie bolken*. Skrifter utgitt av Det Norske Videnskaps-Akademi i Oslo, II. Hist.-Filos. Klasse. 1941. No. 1. Oslo.

Höskuldur Þráinsson 1981. 'Stuðlar, höfuðstafir, hljóðkerfi'. In *Afmæliskveðja til Halldórs Halldórssonar 13. júlí 1981*, 110–23. Reykjavík.

Höskuldur Þráinsson 1982. 'Bölvuð talvan'. *Íslenskt mál og almenn málfræði* 4, 293–94. Reykjavík.

Höskuldur Þráinsson and Kristján Árnason 1984. 'Um reykvísku'. *Íslenskt mál og almenn málfræði* 6, 113–34. Reykjavík.

Höskuldur Þráinsson and Kristján Árnason 1986. 'Um skagfirsku'. *Íslenskt mál og almenn málfræði* 8, 31–62. Reykjavík.

Ingólfur Pálmason 1983. 'Athugun á framburði nokkurra Öræfinga, Suðursveitunga og Hornfirðinga'. *Íslenskt mál og almenn málfræði* 5, 29–51. Reykjavík.

Islands grammatiske litteratur i middelalderen I–II, 1884–1886 (i.e., Samfund til udgivelse af gammel nordisk litteratur XVI (1886) (= vol. I) and XII (1884) (= vol. II)). Copenhagen.

Islandske originaldiplomer indtil 1450. Tekst, 1963. Editiones Arnamagnæanæ A 6. Ed. Stefán Karlsson. Copenhagen.

Jakob Benediktsson 1953. 'Arngrímur lærði og íslenzk málhreinsun'. In *Afmæliskveðja til próf. dr. phil. Alexanders Jóhannessonar háskólarektors 15. júlí 1953 frá samstarfsmönnum og nemendum*, 117–38. Reykjavík.

Jakob Benediktsson 1960a. 'Kvæðabók séra Gissurar Sveinssonar, AM 147, 8vo'. *Íslenzk tunga. Tímarit um íslenzka og almenna málfræði* 2, 159–61 [review]. Reykjavík.

Jakob Benediktsson 1960b. 'Um tvenns konar framburð á ld í íslenzku'. *Íslenzk tunga. Tímarit um íslenzka og almenna málfræði* 2, 32–50. Reykjavík.

Jakob Benediktsson 1964. 'Þættir úr sögu íslenzks orðaforða'. In *Þættir um íslenzkt mál*, 88–109. Reykjavík.

Jóhannes L. L. Jóhannsson 1922. 'Söguleg lýsing íslenzkrar réttritunar um rúmt hundrað ára síðustu'. Offprint from *Skólablaðið*. Reykjavík.

Jóhannes L. L. Jóhannsson 1924. *Nokkrar sögulegar athuganir um helztu hljóðbreytingar o. fl. í íslenzku, einkum í miðaldarmálinu (1300–1600)*. Reykjavík.

Jóhannes L. L. Jóhannsson 1929. 'Nútíðarnafn tungunnar, sem eddukvæðin og fornsögurnar eru ritaðar á'. In *Studier tillägnade Axel Kock*, 134–44. Lund.

Jón Helgason 1926a. *Jón Ólafsson frá Grunnavík* (Safn Fræðafjelagsins um Ísland og Íslendinga V). Copenhagen.

Jón Helgason 1926b. 'Ortografien i AM 350 fol.'. *Meddelelser fra Norsk forening for Sprogvidenskap* I, 45–75. Oslo.

Jón Helgason 1927. 'Anmälan' [review of Björn K. Þórólfsson, *Um íslenskar orðmyndir*]. *Arkiv för nordisk filologi* 43, 88–95. Lund.
Jón Helgason 1928. *Hrappseyjarprentsmiðja 1773–1794* (Safn Fræðafjelagsins um Ísland og Íslendinga VII). Copenhagen.
Jón Helgason 1929. *Málið á Nýja testamenti Odds Gottskálkssonar* (Safn Fræðafjelagsins um Ísland og Íslendinga VII). Reykjavík.
Jón Helgason 1931. 'Från Oddur Gottskálksson till Fjölnir. Tre hundra års isländsk språkutveckling'. In *Island. Bilder från gammal och ny tid*. Skrifter utgivna av Samfundet Sverige–Island 1, 36–50. Lund.
Jón Helgason, ed., 1942. *Arngrímur Jónsson, Gronlandia 1688* (Monumenta Typographica Islandica VI). Copenhagen.
Jón Helgason 1954. 'Hrein íslenzka og miður hrein'. In *Språkvård. Redogörelser och studier utgivna till språkvårdsnämndens tioårsdag*. Skrifter utgivna av Nämnden för svensk Språkvård 11, 95–118. Stockholm. (Reprinted 1959 in *Ritgerðakorn og ræðustúfar* [the *Festschrift* presented to Jón Helgason on his sixtieth birthday by Félag íslenskra stúdenta í Kaupmannahöfn], 216–30. Reykjavík.)
Jón Helgason, ed., 1955a. *Kvæðabók úr Vigur, AM 148, 8vo* (Íslenzk rit síðari alda, 2. flokkur, 1. bindi B). Copenhagen.
Jón Helgason, ed., 1955b. *The Saga Manuscript 2845 4to in the Old Royal Collection in the Royal Library of Copenhagen* (Manuscripta Islandica 2). Copenhagen.
Jón Helgason 1958. *Handritaspjall*. Reykjavík.
Jón Helgason 1960. 'Fem islandske ordsamlinger fra 18. og 19. århundrede'. *Opuscula* I (Bibliotheca Arnamagnæana XX), 271–99. Copenhagen.
Jón Helgason 1970. 'Om islandsk n og nn i tryksvag udlyd'. *Opuscula* IV (Bibliotheca Arnamagnæana XXX), 356–60. Copenhagen.
Jón Aðalsteinn Jónsson 1953. 'Lítil athugun á skaftfellskum mállýzkuatriðum'. In *Afmæliskveðja til próf. dr. phil. Alexanders Jóhannessonar háskólarektors 15. júlí 1953 frá samstarfsmönnum og nemendum*, 139–150. Reykjavík.
Jón Aðalsteinn Jónsson 1959. 'Ágrip af sögu íslenzkrar stafsetningar'. *Íslenzk tunga. Tímarit um íslenzka og almenna málfræði* 1, 71–119. Reykjavík.
Jón Aðalsteinn Jónsson 1964. 'Íslenzkar mállýzkur'. In *Þættir um íslenzkt mál*, 65–87. Reykjavík.
Jón Hilmar Jónsson 1979. *Das Partizip Perfect der schwachen ja-Verben. Die Flexionsentwicklung im Isländischen*. Monographien zur Sprachwissenschaft 6. Heidelberg.
Jón Þorkelsson 1863. *Um r og ur í niðrlagi orða og orðstofna í íslenzku*. Reykjavík.
Jón Þorkelsson 1887. *Breytingar á myndum viðtengingarháttar í fornnorsku og forníslensku*. Reykjavík.
Jón Þorkelsson 1888–1894. *Beyging sterkra sagnorða í íslensku*. Reykjavík.
Jónas Kristjánsson, ed., 1964. *Viktors saga og Blávus* (Riddarasögur II). Reykjavík.
Karker, Allan, 1977. 'The disintegration of the Danish tongue'. In *Sjötíu ritgerðir helgaðar Jakobi Benediktssyni 20. júlí 1977*, 481–90. Reykjavík.
Kjartan G. Ottósson 1983. 'Talva, valva og wōn-stofnar'. *Íslenskt mál og almenn málfræði* 5, 178–83. Reykjavík.
Kjartan G. Ottósson 1987. 'An archaising aspect of Icelandic purism: The revival of extinct morphological patterns'. In *The Nordic Languages and Modern*

Linguistics 6. Proceedings of the Sixth International Conference of Nordic and General Linguistics in Helsinki, August 18–22, 1986, 311–24. Helsinki.

Kjartan G. Ottósson 1990. *Íslensk málhreinsun. Sögulegt yfirlit* (Rit Íslenskrar málnefndar 6). Reykjavík.

Kjartan G. Ottósson 1992. *The Icelandic Middle Voice. The morphological and phonological development.* Lund.

Klemens Jónsson 1930. *Fjögur hundruð ára saga prentlistarinnar á Íslandi.* Reykjavík.

Kock, Axel, 1895. 'Studier i fornnordisk grammatik'. *Arkiv för nordisk filologi* 11, 117–53. Lund.

[Konráð Gíslason] 1836. 'Þáttur um stafsetníng. 1'. *Fjölnir* 2, I, 3–37. Copenhagen.

[Konráð Gíslason] 1837. 'Þáttur um stafsetníng. 2'. *Fjölnir* 3, I, 5–18. Copenhagen.

[Konráð Gíslason] 1844. 'Um stafsetninguna á þessu ári Fjölnis'. *Fjölnir* 7, 1–3. Copenhagen.

Kristján Árnason 1980a. *Íslensk málfræði, fyrri hluti.* Reykjavík.

Kristján Árnason 1980b. *Íslensk málfræði, seinni hluti.* Reykjavík.

Kristján Árnason 1980c. *Quantity in Historical Phonology. Icelandic and related cases.* Cambridge.

Kristján Árnason and Höskuldur Þráinsson 1983. 'Um málfar Vestur-Skaftfellinga'. *Íslenskt mál og almenn málfræði* 5, 81–103. Reykjavík.

de Leeuw van Weenen, Andrea, ed., 1993. *The Icelandic Homily Book. Perg. 15 4° in The Royal Library, Stockholm* (Íslensk handrit. Icelandic Manuscripts. Series in Quarto III). Reykjavík.

Leijström, Gunnar, 1934. 'Delabialisation i isländska'. *Arkiv för nordisk filologi* 50, 307–34. Lund.

Lindblad, Gustaf, 1952. *Det isländska accenttecknet. En historisk-ortografisk studie.* Lunds Universitets årsskrift. N.F. Avd. 1. Bd. 48. Nr. 1. Lund.

Lindblad, Gustaf, 1954. *Studier i Codex Regius av Äldre Eddan.* Lundastudier i nordisk språkvetenskap 10. Lund.

Magnús Stephensen 1806. *Eptirmæli Átjándu Aldar eptir Krists híngadburd, frá Eykonunni Íslandi. Í þessarar nafni framvørpuð af Magnúsi Stephensen.* Leirárgarðar.

Nanna Ólafsdóttir 1961. *Baldvin Einarsson og þjóðmálastarf hans.* Reykjavík.

Noreen, Adolf, 1923. *Altnordische grammatik I. Altisländische und altnorwegische grammatik (laut- und flexionslehre) unter berücksichtigung des urnordischen.* 4th ed. Halle (Saale) (reprinted 1970 as Alabama Linguistic and Philological Series 19, University of Alabama).

Oddur Einarsson 1971. *Íslandslýsing. Qualiscunque descriptio Islandiae.* Trans. Sveinn Pálsson. Reykjavík.

ONP = Ordbog over det norrøne prosasprog. A dictionary of Old Norse prose. Ed. Helle Degnbol et al. 1995– . Copenhagen.

Orešnik, Janez, 1980. 'On the dental accretion in certain 2nd p. sg. verbal forms of Icelandic, Faroese, and the Old West Germanic languages'. *Íslenskt mál og almenn málfræði* 2, 195–211. Reykjavík.

Ólafur Halldórsson, ed., 1968. *Kollsbók. Codex Guelferbytanus 42. 7. Augusteus Quarto. Inngangur* (Íslenzk handrit. Icelandic Manuscripts. Ser. in Quarto V). Reykjavík.

[Rask, Rasmus], 1828. 'Félagsins ástand og athafnir'. *Skírnir* 2, 36–45. Copenhagen.

Rask, Rasmus, ed., 1830. *Lestrarkver handa heldri manna börnum með stuttum skíríngargreinum um stafrofið og annað þartil heyrandi.* Copenhagen.

Rask, Rasmus, ed., 1832. *Oldnordisk Læsebog indeholdende Prøver af de bedste Sagaer i den gamle islandske Tekst, gjennemset og rettet efter de bedste Oldbøger, samt forsynet med et Ordregister over de vanskeligste Ord.* Copenhagen.

Seelow, Hubert, ed., 1981. *Hálfs saga ok Hálfsrekka.* Reykjavík.

Seip, Didrik Arup, 1955. *Norsk språkhistorie til omkring 1370.* 2nd ed. Oslo.

Stafkrókar. Ritgerðir eftir Stefán Karlsson gefnar út í tilefni af sjötugsafmæli hans 2. desember 1998. 2000 (Stofnun Árna Magnúsonar á Íslandi. Rit 49). Ed. Guðvarður Már Gunnlaugsson. Reykjavík.

Stefán Aðalsteinsson 1987. 'Líffræðilegur uppruni Íslendinga'. In *Íslensk þjóðmenning* I. *Uppruni og umhverfi,* 15–29. Reykjavík.

Stefán Einarsson 1932. 'Um mál á Fljótsdalshéraði og Austfjörðum 1930'. *Skírnir. Tímarit Hins íslenzka bókmenntafélags* CVI, 33–54. Reykjavík.

Stefán Karlsson 1960. *Ortografien i islandske originaldiplomer indtil 1450.* Unpublished Master's thesis, University of Copenhagen.

Stefán Karlsson, ed., 1967. *Sagas of Icelandic Bishops. Fragments of Eight Manuscripts* (Early Icelandic Manuscripts in Facsimile VII). Copenhagen.

Stefán Karlsson 1977. 'Inventio Crucis, cap. 1, og Veraldar saga'. *Opuscula* II:2 (Bibliotheca Arnamagnæana XXV:2), 116–33. Copenhagen. (Also published in *Opuscula Septentrionalia: Festskrift til Ole Widding 10.10.1977,* 116–33. Copenhagen.)

Stefán Karlsson 1978. 'Om norvagismer i islandske håndskrifter'. *Maal og Minne,* 87–101. Oslo. (Reprinted in *Stafkrókar,* 173–87.)

Stefán Karlsson 1979. 'Islandsk bogeksport til Norge i middelalderen'. *Maal og Minne,* 1–17. Oslo. (Reprinted in *Stafkrókar,* 188–204.)

Stefán Karlsson 1981. 'Stafsetning séra Odds á Reynivöllum'. In *Afmæliskveðja til Halldórs Halldórssonar 13. júlí 1981,* 248–84. Reykjavík.

Stefán Karlsson 1982. 'Uppruni og ferill Helgastaðabókar'. In *Helgastaðabók. Nikulás saga. Perg. 4to nr. 16 Konungsbókahlöðu í Stokkhólmi* (Íslensk miðaldahandrit. Manuscripta Islandica Medii Aevi II). Reykjavík.

Stefán Karlsson 1984. 'Um Guðbrandsbiblíu'. *Saga. Tímarit Sögufélags* XXII, 46–55. Reykjavík.

Stefán Karlsson 1985. 'Samfellan í íslensku biblíumáli'. *Bókaormurinn* 14, 14–19. Reykjavík. (Reprinted in *Stafkrókar,* 405–14.)

Stefán Karlsson 1993. 'Samanburður á færeysku og íslensku máli'. In *Frændafundur: fyrirlestrar frá íslensk–færeyskri ráðstefnu í Reykjavík 20.–21. ágúst 1992.* Ed. Magnús Snædal and Turið Sigurðardóttir, 20–31. Reykjavík.

Steingrímur J. Þorsteinsson 1950. 'Íslenzkar biblíuþýðingar'. *Víðförli. Tímarit um guðfræði og kirkjumál* 4, 48–85. Reykjavík.

Sveinn Bergsveinsson 1955. 'Þróun ö-hljóða í íslenzku'. In Studia Islandica 14, 5–39. Reykjavík.

Two Versions of Snorra Edda from the 17th Century. 1977–79. Vol. I: *Edda Magnúsar Ólafssonar (Laufás Edda);* Vol. II: *Edda Islandorum. Völuspá. Hávamál. P. H. Resen's editions of 1665.* Ed. Anthony Faulkes. Reykjavík.

Veturliði Óskarsson 2003. *Middelnedertyske låneord i islandsk diplomsprog frem til år 1500* (Bibliotheca Arnamagnæana XLIII). Copenhagen.
Vilhjálmur Þ. Gíslason 1923. *Íslensk endurreisn. Tímamótin í menningu 18. og 19. aldarinnar.* Reykjavík.
Vilhjálmur Þ. Gíslason 1926. *Eggert Ólafsson. Íslensk endurreisn, önnur bók.* Reykjavík.
de Vries, Jan, 1962. *Altnordisches etymologisches Wörterbuch.* Leiden.
Walter, Ernst, 1976a. 'Einige mit *sam-* präfigierte Komposita in früher altwestnordischer Überlieferung'. *Nordeuropa. Studien* 9. *Wissenschaftliche Zeitschrift der Ernst-Moritz-Arndt-Universität Greifswald,* 103–14. Greifswald.
Walter, Ernst, 1976b. *Lexicalisches Lehngut im Altwestnordischen. Untersuchungen zum Lehngut im etisch-moralischen Wortschatz der frühen lateinischaltwestnordischen Übersetzungsliteratur.* Abhandlungen der sächsischen Akademie der Wissenschaften zu Leipzig. Philologisch-historische Klasse, Band 66, Heft 2. Berlin.
van Weenen, Andrea de Leeuw. See (de) Leeuw van Weenen, Andrea.
Westergård-Nielsen, Chr., 1946. *Låneordene i det 16. århundredes trykte islandske litteratur* (Bibliotheca Arnamagnæana VI). Copenhagen.
Widding, Ole, 1961. 'Conscientia i norrøne oversættelser'. *Opuscula* II:1 (Bibliotheca Arnamagnæana XXV:1), 48–51. Copenhagen.
Þættir um íslenzkt mál eftir nokkra íslenzka málfræðinga. 1964. Ed. Halldór Halldórsson. Reykjavík.

General index

NOTE. This index covers proper names and a selection of descriptive terms used in the text. The alphabetical order is the same as that in the Bibliography. Icelanders are listed by their first names.

Alþingi 64
analogy, analogical forms, etc. 14, 15, 18, 21, 22, 25, 26, 27, 29, 48
Anglo-Norman 33
apocope 16, 22
Ari, fifteenth-century priest 50, 51
Arnamagnæan Foundation 36–37
Arngrímur Jónsson 'the learned' (1568–1648) 36, 57
Arnkell Guðvarðsson (16th century), witness to a deed of gift in Svarfaðardalur 52, 53
Atlantic, the 8
Álftafjörður 54, 55
Árni Magnússon (1663–1730) 36, 55
Ásbrandur Þorleiksson 44, 45
Baldvin Einarsson (1801–33) 37
Beitistaðir, in Leirársveit 58
Bessastaðir, on Álftanes 37
Bevers saga 48
Bible, the 28, 34
Björn Jónsson (1846–1912), newspaper editor and government minister 63
Björn Magnússon Ólsen (1850–1919), university professor 63
Black Death, the 48, 49
black letter (script), *see* Gothic script
breaking 8, 25
Bremen, Germany 39
British Isles, the 8
Búnaðarbálkur, poem by Eggert Ólafsson (*q.v.*) 56
Byzantium 31
Celtic 8, 9, 31
Celts 9
chivalric culture, *see* European chivalric culture
Christian literature 34; Christian missions 32
Christianity 7, 32
Church, the 32, 33, 34, 39; the Icelandic Church 39
combinative change(s) 7, 13, 14, 18–19, 46, 47, 50
compound words 16
contraction 27
conversion (to Christianity), the 7, 32
Copenhagen 34, 35, 37, 57
Crymogæa, by Arngrímur Jónsson (*q.v.*) 36
Dalir, *see* Hvammur í Dölum
Danes 37
Danicisms 35
Danish 7, 8, 10, 33, 34, 35, 36, 37, 38, 53, 54; 'Danish tongue' 9
Denmark 23, 33, 34, 58
dialect(s), dialectal differences, etc. 7, 18, 20, 23–24, 64, 65, 66
digraphs 40
dual number, the 28
'dǫnsk tunga' ('Danish tongue') 9
East Scandinavian 8, 39
eastern Iceland [*Austurland*] 13, 22
Edda, *see* Snorri Sturluson
Eggert Ólafsson (1726–68), deputy lawman and poet 37, 56, 57, 58
Egypt 41
Ein ny Psalma Bok, Guðbrandur Þorlákssonʼs hymnal 52
elision 16
English, the 9
Enlightenment, the 37, 51
epenthetic u 15, 30, 47, 59, 62
European chivalric culture 33
Faroes, the 23, 34
Faroese 23
Finnish 8
First Grammarian, the 41, 45
First Grammatical Treatise, the 7, 9, 10, 40, 41, 44

Fjölnir, periodical 37, 38, 60, 61, 62
flámæli 'open-mouthed speech' 13
fornaldarsögur, see sagas of antiquity
French 33, 59
German 33, 34, 36, 37, 59; North German vernacular writings 39
Germanic 8, 32
Germans 33
Gothic (i.e., black letter) script 59, 60
Grammar School, the [*Hinn lærði skóli*], in Reykjavík 61
Greek 32; the Greek aphabet 41
Gronlandia, by Arngrímur Jónsson (*q.v.*) 57
Guðbrandur Þorláksson (*c*.1542–1627), Bishop of Hólar 34, 51, 52, 55
Gunnarr Hámundarson, of Hlíðarendi 44, 45
Halldór Kr. Friðriksson (1819–1902), head teacher 61–63
Hallgerðr langbrók Höskuldsdóttir, of Hlíðarendi 44, 45
Hallgrímur Pétursson (*c*.1614–74), pastor and poet 36
Hamburg, Germany 39
Hamburg–Bremen, archdiocese of 39
Hannes Finnsson (1739–96), Bishop of Skálholt 37
harðmæli 'hard speech' 17, 22
Heimskringla 42
Helga Þorgrímsdóttir from Ingjaldshóll 50, 51
Helgeå, river in Skåne (Scania) 42, 43
hiatus 15, 16
Hið íslenska bókmenntafélag, *see* Icelandic Literary Society, the
hljóðvilla 'sound-confusion' 13
homilies 32
honorific forms 28
Hornafjörður 54, 55
Hólar, in Hjaltadalur 58
Hrappsey, island off Skarðsströnd 58
Hússpostilla, book of sermons by Jón Þorkelsson Vídalín (*q.v.*) 54
Hvammur í Dölum, in Hvammssveit 55

Iceland 8, 33, 34, 36, 64, 65
Icelanders 9, 32–33, 35–36, 38–40, 47, 51, 64, 66
Icelanders, sagas of [= *Íslendinga sögur*, family sagas] 35
Icelandic Bible Society, the [*Hið íslenska Biblíufélag*] (1815–) 34
Icelandic Homily Book, the 66
Icelandic Literary Society, the (Hið íslenska bókmenntafélag, 1816–) 60, 61
Illugi (15th century), recipient of a heifer 50, 51
Indo-European language family, the 8
isolative changes 46
Íslensk fornrit series 41
Jews 41
'journalists' spelling', the 63
Jón Guðmundsson (15th century), recipient of homespun cloth 50, 51
Jón Oddsson (16th century), of Svarfaðardalur 52, 53
Jón Ólafsson (1705–79) from Grunnavík, scholar 36, 56
Jón Ólafsson (1850–1916), newspaper editor 63
Jón Sigurðsson (1811–79), president of the Icelandic Literary Society (*q.v.*) 60
Jón Þorkelsson Vídalín (1666–1720), Bishop of Skálholt 36, 37, 54
Jónas Hallgrímsson (1807–45), poet 37
Jónsbók 35–36, 46
Ketill Jörundsson (1603–70), parson at Hvammur í Dölum 55, 56
Ketilríðr Hólmkelsdóttir of Foss 50, 51
kings' sagas 35
Knútr [Sveinsson] (= Cnut the Great, d. 1035), king of the Danes 42, 43
Konráð Gíslason (1808–91), university professor 37, 60, 61
Konungsskuggsjá 58
Kringla (= Lbs. fragm. 82) 42
Landsuppfræðingarfélag [= *Hið íslenska landsuppfræðingarfélag*], *see* Society for National Education
Latin 32, 39, 44

Lærdómslistafélag [= *Hið íslenska lærdómslistafélag*], see Learned Arts Society
Learned Arts Society, the [Icelandic] [= *Hið íslenska lærdómslistafélag*] 37, 58
Leirárgarðar, in Leirársveit 58
ligatures, ligatured characters 40, 41, 43, 49, 51
linmæli 'soft speech' 22
loan-translations 36
loan-words 7, 8, 21, 31, 36, 38
Low German 7, 33
Lund, in Skåne (Scania) 39
Magnús Ólafsson (1573–1636), parson at Laufás 35
Magnús Ólafsson Stephensen (1762–1833), judge 37, 58
Mary, the Virgin 50, 51
Middle Ages 33
middle voice 30, 31, 56, 57, 58
mutated forms 31, 39; mutated vowels 40, 41; mutation 8, 15, 25, 40
neologisms 7, 25, 36, 37, 38, 66
New Testament 9, 34, 53
Njáls saga 44, 60
Nordic philology, 37
'Nordic tongue' 9
'norrœn tunga' ('Nordic tongue'), *norræna*, *norræna* ('(Old) Norse') 9
Norse 53, 63; *see also* '(Old) Norse'
North Germanic 8
North German vernacular writings, *see* German
North Germans, *see* Germans
northern Iceland [*Norðurland*] 16, 22
Northern languages 8, 23
Norway 8, 9, 23, 32, 33, 34, 43, 44, 47–48
Norwegian 7, 8, 9, 23, 33, 43, 47, 48, 57
Norwegians 9, 34, 48
Oddur Einarsson (1559–1630), Bishop of Skálholt 36
Oddur Gottskálksson (d. 1556) of Reykir in Ölfus, lawman 9, 34, 53
Oddur Oddsson (*c*.1565–1649), parson at Reynivellir 56

Olavius, i.e., Ólafur Ólafsson, *c*.1741–88, customs officer and editor of *Njáls saga* 60
Old English 32
'(Old) Norse' 9
Old Saxon 32
Old Scandinavian 23
Ólafur Hjaltason (*c*.1500–690), Bishop of Hólar and witness to a deed of gift 52, 53
Ólof geisli Þórisdóttir of Ingjaldshóll 50, 51
patronymics 24, 52
Persian 31
personal names 21, 24, 46, 54, 59, 61
Peter, Saint 50, 51
place-names 16; cf. 22
Proto-Scandinavian 8, 17
purism, purist policy, purists, etc 7, 36, 37
quantity shift, the 12–13, 14, 23
Rask, Rasmus Christian (1787–1832), philologist 35, 59–62
Red Sea, the 41
Reformation, the 7, 33, 34, 35, 49, 65; Reformers 34
Reykjabók (AM 468 4to) 44
Reykjavík (*see also* Grammar School, and University of Iceland) 20, 35, 58, 61
riddarasögur, *see* romances
rímur 35
roman alphabet, the 7, 39; roman capitals 41; roman script 59
romances (*riddarasögur*) 33, 35
Romantic Movement, the 37
runes, the runic alphabet 8, 40
sagas of antiquity (*fornaldarsögur*) 35
sagas of Icelanders 35
saints' lives 32, 35
Scandinavia 23, 61
Scandinavian language(s), speech, etc. 8, 9, 23, 31, 33
Scandinavian peoples 36; Scandinavians 8

'school spelling', the 61, 62, 63
Skaftafellssýsla 9
Skálholt, in Biskupstungur 57
Slavonic 31
Snorri Sturluson's *Edda* 35
Society for National Education, the [Icelandic] [= *Hið íslenska landsuppfræðingarfélag*] (1777–96) 58
Sorø, in Sjælland, Denmark 58
south-eastern Iceland [*Suðausturland*] 14, 21
south-western Iceland [*Suðvesturland*] 13
Stefán Ólafsson (c.1619–88), parson at Vallanes 54
Svarfaðardalur, *see also* Ytra-Hvarf and Ytra-Garðshorn 52, 53
Sveinbjörn Egilsson (1791–1852), headmaster 37
Sweden 33
Swedish 8
syncope 8, 22, 27
Trausti Þorgrímsson of Ingjaldshóll 50, 51
u-mutation 15, 48

'Um brullaupsreið Hornfirðinga', poem by Stefán Ólafsson (*q.v.*) 54
University of Copenhagen 37
University of Iceland [*Háskóli Íslands*], Reykjavík 63
Úlfr Þorgilssson (d. 1027), earl in Denmark 42, 43
Varangian Guard, the 31
Veraldarsaga 40
Vestfirðir 14, 24, 54
Viðey, island in Gullbringusýsla 58
Vikings 31
Vídalín, *see* Jón Þorkelsson Vídalín
Víglundar saga 50
Víglundr Þorgrímsson of Foss 50, 51
Vígslóði, homicide section of the laws 39
West Norwegian 9
West Scandinavian 8, 32
Ytra-Garðshorn in Svarfaðardalur 52, 53
Ytra-Hvarf in Svarfaðardalur 52, 53
Þingeyjarsýsla 24
Þorbrandr Þorleiksson 45
Þorgils Jónsson (16th century), priest 52, 53

Index of words and phrases

NOTE. This index covers words and phrases used in the text as examples of one aspect or another of the Icelandic language. It does not include words contained in the illustrative passages printed and translated below the text of pp. 38–63. Oblique, finite and variant forms are listed only in cases where their occurrences in the text might give rise to doubt as to their dictionary entry forms. The alphabetical order is the same as in the Bibliography.

Danish
automobil 38
befale 33
bil 38
blive 33
magt 33
selskab 33
tænke 33

German
befehlen 33
bleiben 33
denken 33
Gesellschaft 33
Macht 33

Icelandic
aðferð 18
aðrir, *see* annarr
afl 61
agi 50
alin; álnir 13
altari 32
anga 20
annarr, 20–21; aðrir 20
Arason 52
arfur 57
á (preposition) 19
álfur 57
áma 12
át (third pers. sg. pret. indic. of *eta*) 17
ával(l)t 61
bak 12
ball 21
banda 13
banka 18
banna 13
barið, barinn, *see* berja
barn 28
be- 34
beinn 26
belgur 20
berast 31
berja 20, 27; barið, barinn 27; berjast 31
bezt 45
bifreið 38
binda 30
biskup 32
bí- 34
bífala 33
bíhaga 34
bíkvæmilegur 34
bíll 38
bjarg 8, 20
bjarga 29
blaðið, blaðit (*blað* with suffixed definite article) 19
blaðka 18
blár 21
blása 30
blessa, bleza 19
blífa 33
blóðga 20
blómgast 20
Blönd(u)ós 16
bogi 14
borginn 29; *see also* einhver
brjóta 8, 30
broddr 19
brot 18–19
bróðir 25
brúður 24
bryti 26
búa 12, 15, 30
búi 15
byrja 59
bændurnir, bændurnar (nom. pl. of *bóndi*, with suffixed definite article) 25

dag(u)rinn (*dag(u)r* with suffixed definite article) 14, 50, 66
deildarnóti 38
deilingarmerki 38
dekra 13
Dímon 8
djákni 32
drekka 60
dveljast 31
dyr 25
dögg 20
dǫnsk tunga, see General Index
Edda, see General Index
efla 19
eftirkomendurnir, eftirkomendurnar (nom. pl. of *eftirkomandi*, with suffixed definite article) 25
Egill 25
Einar(r) 21
einhver: innundir hjá einhverjum 16; koma einhverjum á kné 19; koma einhverjum í opna skjöldu 24; einhverjum er borgið 29
einn 46
eg, ek 19, 29, 30; mig, mik 19, 31
ekki 16
em, see vera
eng 14; cf. 47, 54
engill 32
enn (definite article): enum spǫkustum mǫnnum 28
enni 12
er (= 'is'), see vera
erfa 47
exi, øxi (acc. and dat. forms of *øx*) 11
ér, see (þ)ér
faðir 25
fagr, fagur 15, 47
fara 30; fór 29; fórt 30; farð(u) ekki 16; ferðu, fer þú 30; þú ferð 30
fast 56
fastaeign, fasteign 16
fá (verb) 8, 15, 16; fáa 15
fár (adj.)15, 16
fátæk(u)r 26

fegrð, fegurð 15
féhús, fjós 15
fingurnir, fingurnar (nom. pl. of *fingur*, with suffixed definite article) 25
finna 21
firðirnir, fjörðurnar (nom. pl. of *fjörður*, with suffixed definite article) 24
fíll 31
fjórir 15, 55
fjós, see féhús
Fjölnir, see General Index
fjör 57
flámæli, see General Index
fley(g)ja 22
fluga 47
folk, fólk 13
for- 34
fordjarfa 34
fornaldarsögur, see General Index
fornema 34
fór, see fara
fótur 59
fregna 29
freista 32
freistni 32
fremzt 45
fæturnir, fæturnar (nom. pl. of *fótur*, with suffixed definite article) 25
fölur 26
gamall 26
ganga 59
gata 20
gefa 59
-gerður 24
Gísli 61
gjöf 59
góðr 26
Guðmundar (gen. sg. of *Guðmund(u)r*) 24
Guðmundsdóttir 24
Guðmundsson 24
guðspjall 32
gufa 17
-gunnur 24
gæfa 17, 45, 50

gæska 60
göfga 20
gǫfugr 27
göltur 59
hafa 17, 18, 19, 20, 42, 47, 52
halmr, hálmr 13
hals, háls 13
hanga 17
hanki 17
hann 29, 30
harðmæli, see General Index
hár; hær(r)i 21
heiði 24
heilagr, heilagur 27
helgi 24
helgur 27
hellir 24
hendurnar (nom. pl. of hönd, with suffixed definite article) 25
hengja 20
-hildur 24
hjá 16
hjálpa 17, 29
hlaupa 48
hleypa 18
hljóðvilla, see General Index
hné, see kné
hnöttur 19
holt 13
hólpinn 29
hreinn (= 'pure') 26
hrinda 29
hross 48
hræddr 12
hugargrip 38
hugr 33
hugskot 33
hugtak 38
hugvit 33
hundrat 47
hver, hvur (pronoun) 15, 54, 61
hvernig, hvurninn 15
hvetja 27
hvolfa 15
hvolpur 15
hvur, see hver
hvurninn, see hvernig
hylja 20
hærri (comp. of hár), see hár
hǫfn 23
inn(i)undir 16; see also einhver
innri, iðri 21
it (pronoun), see (þ)it
í 24
ís(s) 21
Íslenzk fornrit, see General Index
Jónsbók, see General Index
kall, see karl
kalla 27, 48; kallask 30–31
karl, kall 46
kálfar (nom. pl. of kálf(u)r) 19
kemba 20
kenna 59, 61
Ketill 59
kippa 19–20
kirkja 32
Kjartan 8
kjör, kør (= 'choice') 17, 45, 57
klaret 33
klaustr 32
kné, hné 19; see also einhver
knör(r) 21
knöttur 19
kol 19
kollr 19
koma 19, 24, 30, 50
konan (kona with suffixed definite article) 52
Konungskuggsjá, see General Index
kurteisi 33
kurteiss 33
kveðja (verb) 27
kváðu (third pers. pl. pret. indic. of kveða) 14
kvíga 60
kvöld 15, 54
kyrr 11
kǫr, kör (= '(sick)bed') 17
kør (= 'choice'), see kjör
lagðr, see leggja

land 61
langur 66
lauss 26
láta 8
leggja 18, 27; lagðr 27
lepja 13
lesa 30
linmæli, see General Index
Litl(ih)amar 16
ljósta 30
Loftur 61
lygi 14
lykill 25, 52
lærisveinn 28
lögin (lög with suffixed definite article) 14
maðr 20, 21, 28, 48; maðurinn 52; mann 28; manninn 52; mǫnnum 28, 48; mannum 48
makt 33
malr 10
mann, manninn, see maðr
mál 10
máttugur 20
mega 14
melr 10
miður 26
mig, mik, see ek, eg
min(n)zt 45
mjeg, see mjög
mjólk 16, 18
mjög, mjeg 15, 55; mjök 19
morgunn 22
móðir 25
mælir (noun) 24
mǫnnum, see maðr
nafn 19
nakkvarr, see nokkur(r)
nástund 38
negla 20
nekkverr, see nokkur(r)
Njáll 8
nokkur(r), nokkuð; nakkvarr, nekkverr, nökkurr 29
'norrœn tunga', norræna, norrœna, see General Index

nútíð 38
nýr 26
nökkurr, see nokkur(r)
obláta 32
Oddný 46
okkarr 28
opinn 24, 27; see also einhver
opna 17
orð 61
orf 19
organ 33
ostur 56
óðr 24
ófjeti 15
ófjöt 15
óheppinn 61
Palli 21
pansari 33
Páll 21
prestr 32
reka 12
riddarasögur, see General Index
rita, ríta 29
rík(u)r 18, 26
rímur, see General Index
rjúka 62
róa 15
röskur 26
saga 18, 47
sagði, see segja
samviska 32–33
segja 18, 20, 29, 61; segi(r) 29, 30; segir 22, seigir, seier 50; sagða 29; sagði 20, 29
seldr (pp. of selja) 12
selskapur 33
semja 20
sess 21
séa, see sjá (verb)
séður, sénn (pp. of sjá) 29
Sigurðar (gen. sg. of Sigurð(u)r) 24
Sigurðardóttir 24
Sigurðsson 24
silki 33
sígaretta 38
sjá (verb) 8, 15, 29; séa 15

sjá (pronoun) 28
sje, see sjö
sjö, sje 15
skarlat 33
Skálaholt, Skálholt 16
skelfa 20
skjöldur 24; see also einhver
Skógar 22
slafak 9
sleppa 18
smiðr 23
smjer, smjör 15
sofn 9
sofnhús 9
sonu, see synir
spakur 62; spakari, spakastr 28
spekt, spekþ 20
spyrja 11, 27
spyrjandi, spyrjanda (present participle of spyrja) 28
stampur 18
steði, steðji 26
stigi 14
stjel 15
stjölr 15
stór(r) 21
stökkva 18 (weak), 62 (strong)
suðr 20
sunnan 21
synd 32
synir, sonu (nom. and acc. pl. of son(u)r) 24
systir 25
svá, svo 14
sváfu (third pers. pl. pret. indic. of sofa) 14
söngur 25
tala (verb) 17
tekr (third pers. sg. pres. indic. of taka) 59
teljast 60
torg 31
tvisvar 13
tvöfaldur 15
týndr (pp. of týna) 12
tölva 25

ulfr, úlfr 13
ungr 14
uppgötva 13
uppi 17
urð 13
urr 13
vaka 17
vala 25
vald 45
valda 13
valdi, valði, see velja
valva, see völva
vanta 18
vatn 22
vaxa 48
vá (noun) 14; cf. 47, 54, 59
váði, voði 14
várr, vor 28
vega 61
veiði 24
velja; valði, valdi 45
venja (verb) 20
vera 30; em 30; er 29, 30
verða 48
veturnir, veturnar (nom. pl. of vetur, with suffixed definite article) 25
vélindi, vælindi 14
vér, vær 14, 28
við, vit (pronoun) 19
vili, vilji 26
vinda 38
vindast 22
vindhraði 22
vindill 38
vindlingur 38
vindstig 22
vinnast 22
viska 60
vit (dual pronoun) 19, 28
Vígslóði, see General Index
von 59
vonska 60
vor, see várr
völva, valva 25
y(ð)varr 28
ykkarr 28

Yngvildr, Yngveldr, Yngvöldur 55
þanki 52
þekkur 62
þenkja 33
þessi 29
(þ)ér 28
þing 47
(þ)it 28
þolinmóðr 32
þolinmœði 32
þorn 40
þurs 40
þú 30
þvá, þvo 29

þveginn (pp. of *þvá, þvo*) 29
æður 24
ægir 50
ærinn 61
ögn 20
ör (noun) 25
øxi, *see* exi

Latin

conscientia 32
evangelium 32

Old English

godspell 32